21 IoT Experiments

First Edition

Yashavant Kanetkar
Shrirang Korde

FIRST EDITION 2018

Copyright © BPB Publications, INDIA
ISBN :978-93-8655-183-2

All Rights Reserved. No part of this publication can be stored in a retrieval system or reproduced in any form or by any means without the prior written permission of the publishers.

LIMITS OF LIABILITY AND DISCLAIMER OF WARRANTY
The Author and Publisher of this book have tried their best to ensure that the programmes, procedures and functions described in the book are correct. However, the author and the publishers make no warranty of any kind, expressed or implied, with regard to these programmes or the documentation contained in the book. The author and publisher shall not be liable in any event of any damages, incidental or consequential, in connection with, or arising out of the furnishing, performance or use of these programmes, procedures and functions. Product name mentioned are used for identification purposes only and may be trademarks of their respective companies.

All trademarks referred to in the book are acknowledged as properties of their respective owners.

Distributors:

BPB PUBLICATIONS 20,
Ansari Road, Darya Ganj
New Delhi-110002
Ph: 23254990/23254991

BPB BOOK CENTRE
376 Old Lajpat Rai Market,
Delhi-110006
Ph: 23861747

MICRO MEDIA
Shop No 5, Mahendra Chambers, 150 DN Rd. Next to Capital Cinema, V.T. (C.S.T.) Station, MUMBAI-400 001 Ph: 22078296/22078297

DECCAN AGENCIES
4-3-329, Bank Street,
Hyderabad-500195
Ph: 24756967/24756400

Published by Manish Jain for BPB Publications, 20, Ansari Road, Darya Ganj, New Delhi-110002 and Printed him at Repro India Pvt Ltd, Mumbai

Dedicated to
Nalinee and Prabhakar Kanetkar

- *Yashavant Kanetkar*

Dedicated to
H.H. Shri Maibai

- *Shrirang Korde*

About The Authors

Yashavant Kanetkar

Through his books and Quest Video Courseware DVDs on C, Java, C++, Data Structures, VC++, .NET, Embedded Systems, etc. Yashavant Kanetkar has created, moulded and groomed lacs of IT careers in the last two decades. Yashavant's books and Quest DVDs have made a significant contribution in creating top-notch IT manpower in India and abroad.

Yashavant's books are globally recognized and millions of students / professionals have benefitted from them. Yashavant's books have been translated into Hindi, Gujarati, Japanese, Korean and Chinese languages. Many of his books are published in India, USA, Japan, Singapore, Korea and China.

Yashavant is a much sought after speaker in the IT field and has conducted seminars/workshops at TedEx, IITs, RECs and global software companies.

Yashavant has recently been honored with the prestigious "Distinguished Alumnus Award" by IIT Kanpur for his entrepreneurial, professional and academic excellence. This award was given to top 50 alumni of IIT Kanpur who have made significant contribution towards their profession and betterment of society in the last 50 years.

In recognition of his immense contribution to IT education in India, he has been awarded the "Best .NET Technical Contributor" and "Most Valuable Professional" awards by Microsoft for 5 successive years.

Yashavant holds a BE from VJTI Mumbai and M.Tech. from IIT Kanpur.

Shrirang Korde

Shrirang is a Technology expert in product development with international exposure. His more than two decades of rich experience spans across companies like Bharat Electronics, Tata Elxsi, Philips Software, Persistent Systems and ERP based startup. He was instrumental in starting Technology Incubator at VNIT Nagpur. He has handled various overseas customers including working in countries like Japan, Taiwan, Netherlands and Belgium. His areas of work are DSP/Embedded systems, Telecom Systems, Android Systems and Cloud based Software development.

Shrirang conducts training in various technologies like Java, Android, IoT, Cloud and .NET/C#. He has got two publications to his credit and received various project awards during his work tenure. Shrirang has done his B.E. from VNIT, Nagpur and M.E. from BITS Pilani.

Acknowledgments

Though our name goes on the cover, 21 IoT Experiments is not an outcome of our efforts alone. A book on such an emerging topic requires inputs, help and suggestions from several people, including hands-on experiences of students who participated in our trainings. Their inputs have gone a long way in getting this book in the shape and form in which you are holding it.

Over the years, we have built many applications and all these practical experiences and usage scenarios are factored into 21 IoT Experiments.

We are am indebted to Manish Jain of BPB Publications who had a faith in this book idea, believed in our writing ability, whispered the words of encouragement and made helpful suggestions from time to time. I hope every author gets a publisher who is as cooperative, knowledgeable and supportive as Manish.

We also would like to thank Siddharth Dev of Technido, Indore, India in suggesting the sensors and some experiment ideas.

We also would like to thank www.brainyquote.com for providing such a wonderful collection of quotes. This prompted us to begin every experiment chapter with an apt quote.

We thank our respective families for enduring the late nights, the clicking keyboard and mostly for putting up with yet another marathon book effort.

Experiments

ZERO	IOT KIT OVERVIEW	1
ONE	LED PATTERN	13
TWO	SWITCH BASED LED COUNTER	21
THREE	ANALOG I/O-FADE LEDs USING POTENTIOMETER	31
FOUR	USING MILLIS	39
FIVE	REMOTE CONTROL BASED MELODY PLAYER	47
SIX	USING EEPROM TO CONTROL DEVICES	59
SEVEN	MOTOR SPEED CONTROL	69
EIGHT	ACCELEROMETER BASED ROTATION CONTROL	77
NINE	WIRELESS CONNECTIVITY	97
TEN	SEND EMAIL	107
ELEVEN	DIGITAL CLOCK	123
TWELVE	WAMP SERVER BASED TEMPERATURE LOGGER	133
THIRTEEN	INTERNET / INTRANET BASED LED CONTROL	147
FOURTEEN	INTERNET BASED TEMP. LOGGER WITH TWEETS	159
FIFTEEN	INTERNET BASED HOME AUTOMATION	175
SIXTEEN	STREET LIGHT CONTROL	187
SEVENTEEN	HOME SECURITY SYSTEM	199
EIGHTEEEN	WATER LEVEL MONITOR	211
NINETEEN	MULTICOLOR CONTROL	223
TWENTY	INTERNET BASED MOTOR SPEED CONTROL	237
TWENTY ONE	SOIL MOISTURE MONITOR & SD-CARD LOGGER	249
TWENTY TWO	ARDUINO PINS AND CONCEPTS	259

Preface

For benefiting from this book, we don't expect or assume any Electronics Engineering background from the readers. In our opinion, IoT is an inter-disciplinary field. To become a good IoT developer one needs to grasp the fundamentals of programming, hardware interaction, and technologies like sensors, cloud computing, embedded systems, communication and security. Learning each of these in the context of IoT needs two things—achieving some meaningful task that makes use of the above-mentioned technologies and the hardware on which you can actually try these tasks.

With that motive we have crafted 21 IoT Experiments for you. Each experiment is self-sufficient and has a very clear goal. Not only does each Experiment chapter indicate what hardware to use, and what pin connections to make, it also explains the working of the Experiment sketch in a simple language. The various library functions and their explanations are also included for ready reference. The details of some concepts like PWM, I2C, etc. on which some of the experiments are based have been compiled into a separate chapter at the end of the book. At the end of each Experiment chapter, there is a section called "More Tweaks" to enhance the Experiment with more ideas. Do try them so that you grow in confidence.

Should you need to purchase the IoT hardware needed for performing the experiments along with the videos of each, please fill in the order form given at the end of the book.

Though you can pick and try the experiments in this book in any order; we would suggest you that you rather not. We have arranged the Experiments in a sequence that ensures smooth flow and a steady progression.

We believe that once you perform the various IoT experiments you would gain satisfaction of doing concrete IoT activity along with good learning experience. Lastly, as you work your way through the Experiments, have the tenacity and patience that will make you a true IoT developer.

- Yashavant Kanetkar
- Shrirang Korde

INTRODUCTION
IoT KIT OVERVIEW

There is nothing more difficult to take in hand, more perilous to conduct, or more uncertain in its success, than to take the lead in the introduction of a new order of things.

- Niccolo Machiavelli

IoT Kit Overview

This chapter provides an overview of the KICIT Internet of Things (IoT) kit, Arduino IDE and steps required for Sketch development. This kit is used for all the experiments given in the chapters to follow. Not every experiment would need all the kit components. The KICIT IoT kit components are shown in the Figure 1.1.

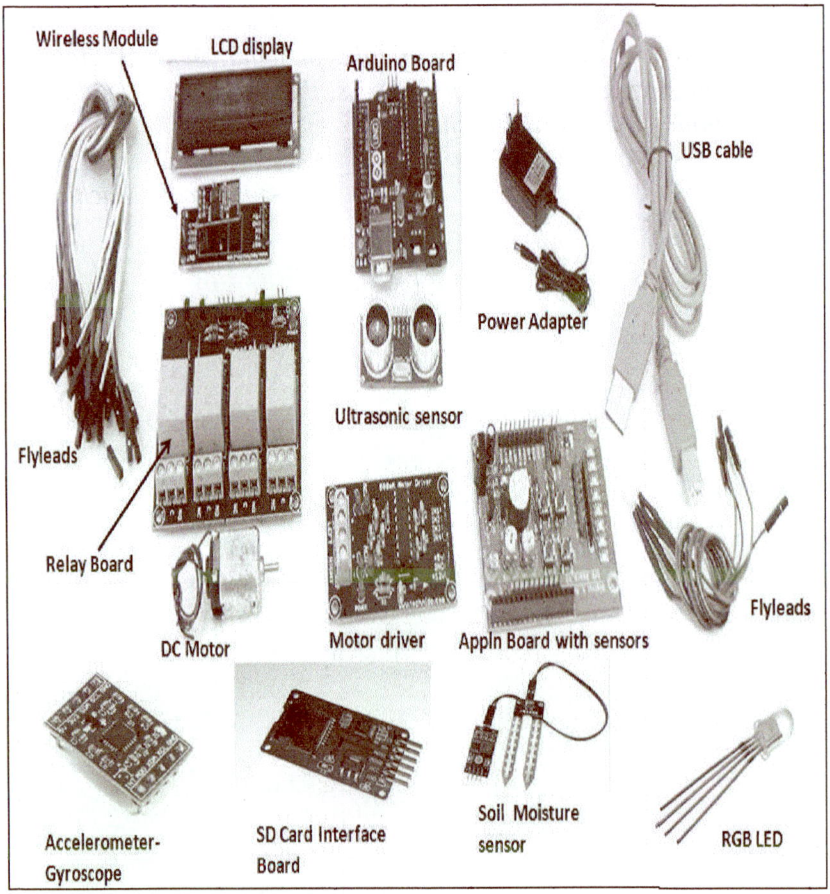

Figure 1.1 IoT Kit components

The KICIT IoT kit contains the following components:
- Arduino Uno with ATMega328 microcontroller

IoT Kit Overview

- WiFi module (ESP-8266 with break out board)
- Power Adapter 9V-12V / Battery holder for 6 cells
- Daughter Boards and Sensors:
    - Liquid Crystal Display (LCD)
    - Application Board (Digital & Analog I/O Board)
    - Multi Colored LED
    - Relay board with 4 relays
    - DC motor
    - Motor Driver board
    - Ultrasonic sensor
    - Accelerometer & Gyroscope
    - SD card
    - Moisture Sensor
    - USB cable

Boards and Sensors

Arduino Board:

Arduino is a prototype platform (open-source) based on an easy-to-use hardware and software. It consists of a circuit board, which can be programmed using software tool called Arduino IDE (Integrated Development Environment). IDE used to write and upload the computer code to the physical board. The capabilities of Arduino Uno board are extended to provide IoT using ESP8266.

ESP8266 with breakout board:

The ESP8266 is a WiFi module suitable for adding WiFi functionality to an existing microcontroller project via a UART serial connection. The module includes:

- 802.11 b/g/n protocol
- Wi-Fi Direct (P2P), soft-AP
- Integrated TCP/IP protocol stack

The ESP 8266 comes with break out board which allows ESP8266 to interface various pins for transmit / receive and power supply with Arduino Uno.

Relay:

A relay is a switch or like a lever which switches on with small current (mA). It switches on another appliance (Bulb, Pump etc) using much bigger current (5 Amp, 240 V).

Soil Moisture Sensor:

The moisture sensor is a simple water sensor used to detect soil moisture. When the soil moisture is in deficit, module outputs a high level. When the soil moisture is substantial, module outputs a low.

Multi Color LED (RGB LED):

Multi Color LED is three LEDs in one i.e. Red, Green and Blue LEDs packed in one casing with a common point.

Temperature Sensor:

The LM35 series are precision integrated-circuit temperature device with an output voltage linearly-proportional to the Centigrade temperature.

Ultrasonic Sensor:

The ultrasonic sensor (HC-SR04) uses sonar to determine distance to an object. This is similar the way in which bats detects object. The sensor offers non-contact range detection with high accuracy and stable readings in an easy-to-use package. Its operation is not affected by sunlight or black material like Sharp rangefinders are (although materials like cloth can be difficult to detect).

Accelerometer & Gyroscope (MPU 6050):

MPU-6050 is single chip Accelerometer & Gyroscope. Accelerometer measures acceleration. It responds to vibrations associated with the movement when an object goes from standstill to any velocity. It measures acceleration on one, two, or three axes. Gyroscope uses earth's gravity to determine orientation. It based on principle of angular momentum and measures the rate of rotation around a particular axis. Accelerometer & Gyroscope senses motion left/ right, up/ down, forward/ backward. It also detects angular moments from three axes X, Y, Z referred as Yaw, Roll, Pitch.

DC Motor with DC motor driver board:

IoT Kit Overview

The DC motor requires a driver board so that it can be properly interfaced and controlled via Arduino Uno. The driver board ensures appropriate current and voltage is provided so that it does not overload Arduino Uno. The driver board has ability to driver two different motors.

IR receiver:

IR receiver (TSOP173x) has a photo detector (which detects IR signals) and preamplifier in one package. It outputs a constant HIGH signal when idle and as it receives data, it inverts (outputs active low). It has high immunity against ambient light.

Arduino Tools

Arduino IDE (Integrated Development Environment) is used for developing sketches. The IDE can be downloaded from the link
https://www.arduino.cc/en/Main/Software

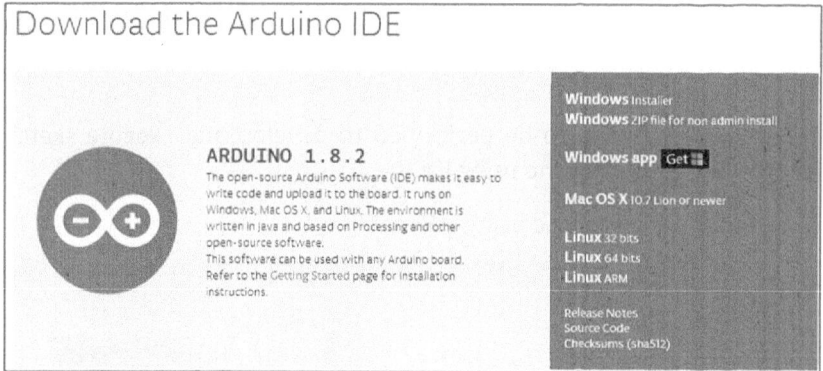

Figure 1.2 Download Arduino IDE

Once downloaded, we need to install it. For this double click to execute "arduino-1.8.x-windows.exe". The Figure 3 shows various installations steps.

6 21 IoT Experiments

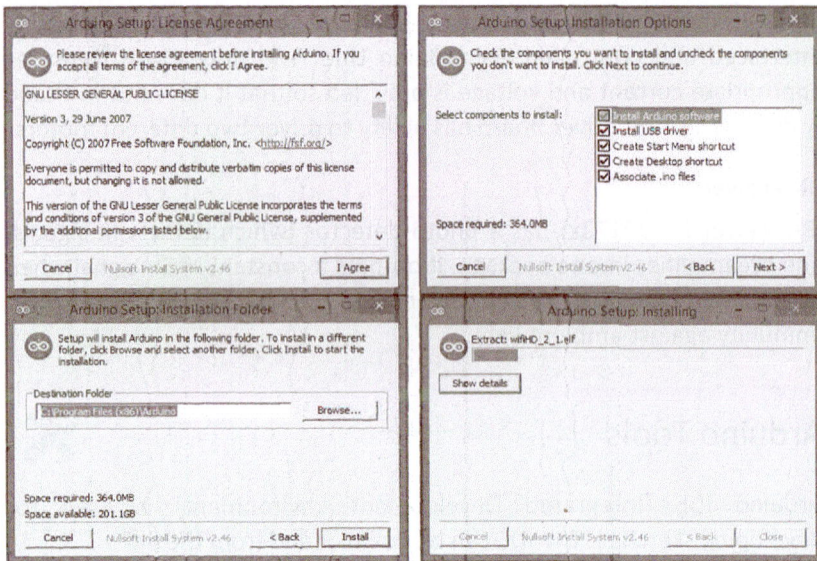

Figure 1.3 Installation steps

Development Steps

Following steps need to be performed to develop and execute sketch (program) on Arduino Uno using IDE:

- **Connect Arduino Uno using USB cable**

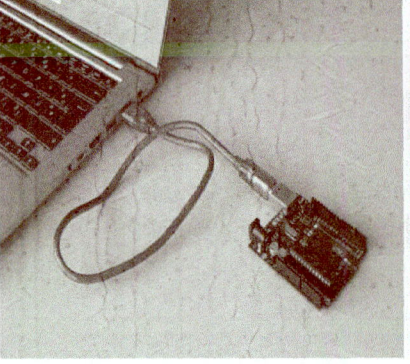

IoT Kit Overview

- **Select Board (Uno) and Port**

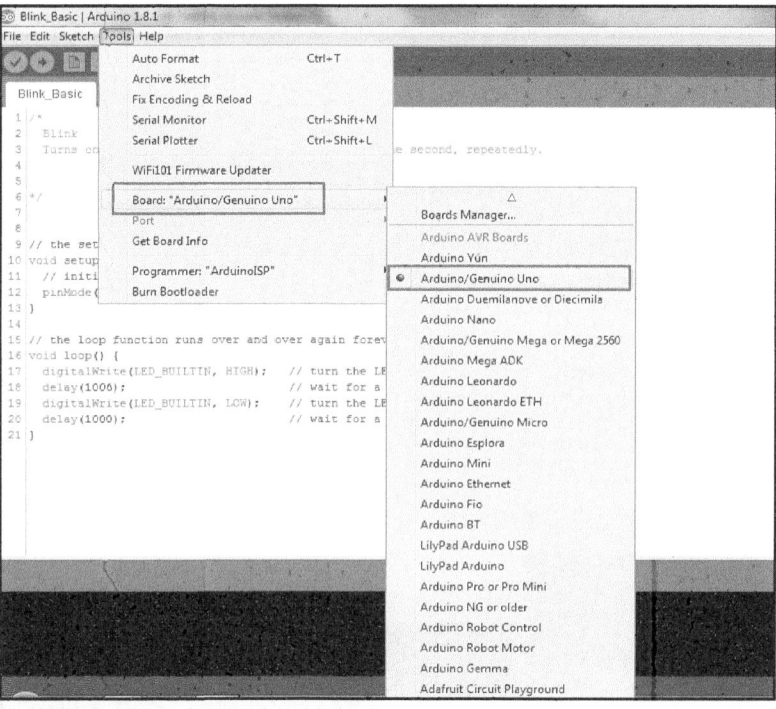

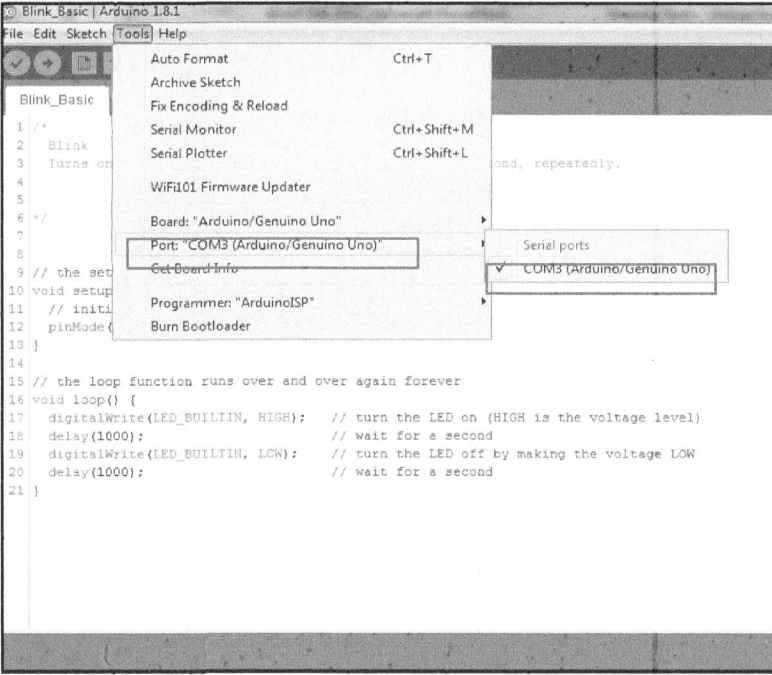

- **Create Sketch** - Add code for the experiment

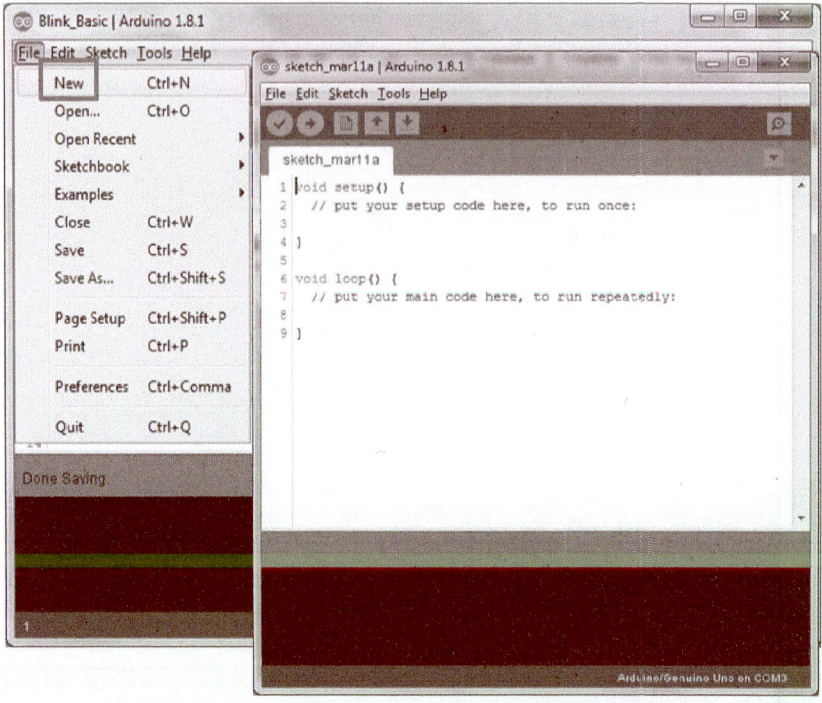

- **Compile the sketch using Verify**

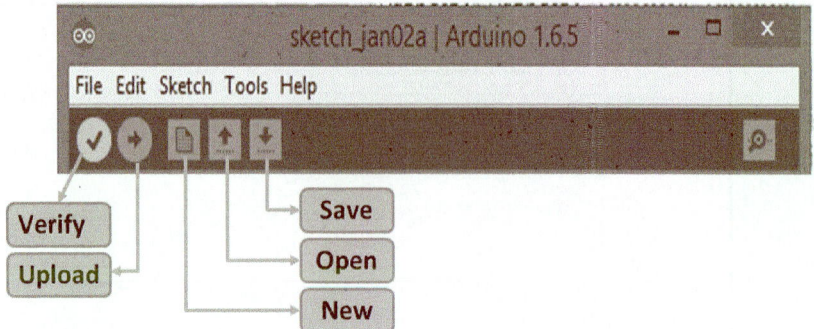

IoT Kit Overview

- **Upload and run**

Detailed Build Process

The previous section mentioned the development steps involved in Arduino programming. You may perform those steps mechanically, but would never get a real hang of things unless you understand the process in detail. This is what this section intends to discuss.

Creating programs for IoT kit Arduino Uno is fundamentally different than creating programs for a PC/Laptop. In the PC/Laptop, the machine that you use to build the program is same as the machine on which you execute it. Unlike this, while building IoT experiments, the program development is done on a PC/Laptop, but its execution is carried out on a different device, in our case the Arduino board. The development PC/Laptop is often known as host and IoT kit boards (Arduino Uno and others) are known as target.

The Arduino environment performs some minor pre-processing to turn a sketch into a C++ program. It then gets passed to a compiler (avr-gcc), which turns the human readable code into machine readable instructions (or object files). Then the code gets combined with (linked against), the standard Arduino libraries that provide basic functions like **digitalWrite( )** or **Serial.print( )**. The result is a single Intel hex file, which contains the specific bytes that need to be written to the program memory of the chip on the Arduino board. This file is then uploaded to the board by transmitting it over the USB or serial connection, via either the bootloader program already present on the chip, or with external programming hardware.

Let us now understand these build steps in detail.

Pre-Processing

The Arduino environment performs a few transformations to the sketch before passing it to the avr-gcc compiler:

- All .ino files in the sketch folder (shown in the IDE as tabs with no extension) are concatenated together and the .cpp extension is added to the filename.

- #include <Arduino.h> is added to the sketch. This header file (found in the core folder for the currently selected board) includes all the definitions needed for the standard Arduino core.

- Prototypes are generated for all function definitions in .ino files that don't already have prototypes. In some rare cases prototype generation may fail for some functions. To work around this, you can provide your own prototypes for these functions.

- #line directives are added to make warning or error messages reflect the original sketch layout.

No pre-processing is done to files in a sketch with any extension other than .ino. Additionally, .h files in the sketch are not automatically #included from the main sketch file. Further, if you want to call functions defined in a .c file from a .cpp file (like one generated from your sketch), you'll need to wrap its declarations in an 'extern "C" { }' block that is defined only inside C++ files.

IoT Kit Overview

Compilation

Sketches are compiled by avr-gcc and avr-g++ according to the variables in the boards.txt file of the selected board's platform.

The sketch is built in a temporary directory in the system-wide temporary directory (e.g. /tmp on Linux).

The .c and .cpp files of the target are compiled and output with .o extensions to this directory, as is the main sketch file and any other .c or .cpp files in the sketch and any .c or .cpp files in any libraries which are #included in the sketch.

Before compiling each .c or .cpp file, an attempt is made to reuse the previously compiled .o file, which speeds up the build process. A special .d (dependency) file provides a list of all other files included by the source. The compile step is skipped if the .o and .d files exist and have timestamps newer than the source and all the dependent files. If the source or any dependent file has been modified, or any error occurs while verifying the files, the compiler is run normally, writing a new .o and .d file. After a new board is selected from the Tools menu, all .c and .cpp files are rebuilt on the next compile.

These .o files are then linked together into a static library and the main sketch file is linked against this library. Only the parts of the library needed for your sketch are included in the final .hex file, reducing the size of most sketches.

The .hex file is the final output of the compilation which is then uploaded to the board.

Uploading

Sketches are uploaded using avrdude. The upload process is also controlled by variables in the boards and main preferences files.

EXPERIMENT ONE

LED PATTERN

"No one ever taught me, and I never had formal classes in pattern making, so I was like, Okay, I'll just drape, and I'll sew as I pin it."

- *Alexander Wang*

Experiment

This Experiment is about glowing LEDs in a pattern. The pattern should be clockwise and anticlockwise (or left to right and right to left). The LEDs should glow from LED1 to LED8 (left to right) and then from LED8 to LED1 (right to left) on the board.

Hardware Setup

This Experiment needs an Arduino Uno board and an Application Board. These are shown in Figure 1.1 and 1.2.

Figure 1.1 Application Board

Experiment 1: LED Patterns **15**

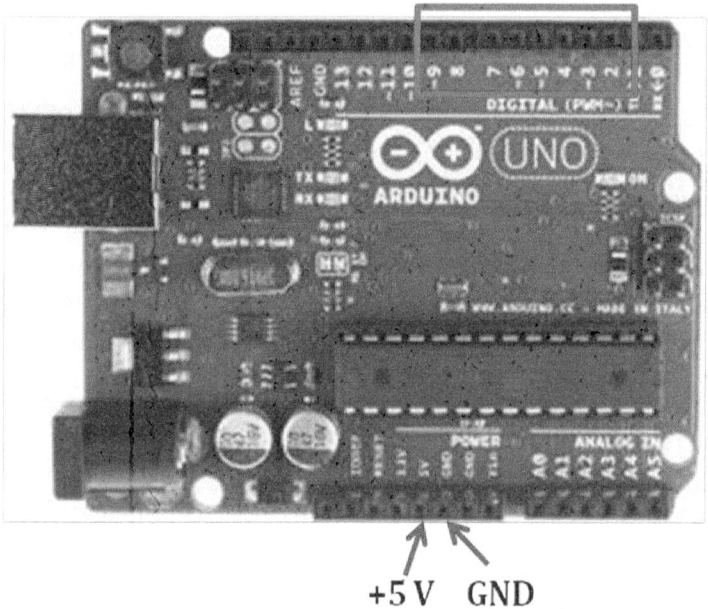

Figure 1.2 Arduino Uno

Pin connections shown in Figure 1.3 should be made.

Arduino Pins	Application Board Pins
+5V	+5V
GND	GND
Digital pin 2	LED1
Digital pin 3	LED2
Digital pin 4	LED3
Digital pin 5	LED4
Digital pin 6	LED5
Digital pin 7	LED6
Digital pin 8	LED7
Digital pin 9	LED8

Figure 1.3 Pin connections

Sketch

// LED Patterns

int delay_dur = 500 ; // delay of 500ms

```
// setup function runs once when you press reset or power the board
void setup( )
{
    int i = 0 ;
    int ledPin = 2 ; // Arduino pins 2 to 9 are used
    for ( i = 0 ; i < 8 ; i++ )
    {
        pinMode ( ledPin, OUTPUT ) ; // set pin in OUTPUT mode
        digitalWrite ( ledPin, HIGH ) ; // Make LED1 to LED8 OFF
        ledPin = ledPin + 1 ;
    }
}

// loop function runs over and over again forever
void loop( )
{
    int i = 0 ;
    int ledPin = 2   ;

    // for loop for left to right LED glow
    for ( i = 0 ; i < 8 ; i++ )
    {
        digitalWrite ( ledPin, LOW ) ;
        delay ( delay_dur ) ;
        digitalWrite ( ledPin, HIGH ) ;
        ledPin = ledPin + 1 ;
        delay ( delay_dur ) ;   // wait
    }
    ledPin-- ;

    // for loop for right to left LED glow
    for ( i = 8 ; i > 0 ; i-- )
    {
        digitalWrite ( ledPin, LOW ) ;
```

Experiment 1: LED Patterns **17**

```
            delay ( delay_dur ) ;
            digitalWrite ( ledPin, HIGH ) ;
            ledPin = ledPin - 1 ;
            delay ( delay_dur ) ;   // wait
    }
}
```

Result

The LEDs glow one by one, from LED1 to LED8 with a delay. It means LED1 glows for delay duration and then it goes off, then LED2 glows for delay duration and it goes off, then LED3 glows, etc. After reaching LED8, this glow pattern reverses from LED8 to LED1.

Explanation

In the **setup( )** function, pins 2 to 9 are configured as OUTPUT pins using **pinMode( )** function. They are set at HIGH level using **digitalWrite( )** function. The pins are made HIGH so that initially all LEDs are off. Setting HIGH gives 5V at each pin and since LEDs (1 to 8) on Application board are already connected to +5V, setting HIGH makes them not to glow. This is done using a **for** loop.

In the **loop( )** function, two **for** loops have been used. First **for** loop glows LEDs one by one from LED1 to LED8. This means that LED1 glows then it is turned off, then LED2 glows and it is turned off. This process continues till LED8. In the second **for** loop LED8 glows and it's turned off, then LED7 glows and it's turned off. This continues till LED1. Both the loops make use of the following functions:

digitalWrite (ledpin, LOW) ;
digitalWrite (ledpin, HIGH) ;

When LOW is passed to **digitalWrite( )** LED glows as setting LOW allows the current to flow through LED. When HIGH is passed, LED turns off, as setting HIGH does not let the current flow through LED.

A variable **ledpin** is used to control a pin. After end of the first **for** loop, **ledpin** is 10, hence before start of second **for** loop its value is decremented using **ledpin--**.

Functions Used

Given below is a list of functions that have been used in this Experiment's sketch.

pinMode (pin, mode)
Configures the specified pin to behave either as input or as output.
pin is the number of the pin whose mode needs to be set.
mode can be INPUT, OUTPUT, or INPUT_PULLUP.
It is possible to enable the internal pullup resistors with the mode INPUT_PULLUP. The INPUT mode explicitly disables the internal pullups.
digitalWrite (pin, value)
Outputs either logical level HIGH or LOW
pin can be specified as either a variable or constant.
When the pin is configured as OUTPUT, its voltage is set to the corresponding values—5V for HIGH, 0V (ground) for LOW.
When the pin is configured as INPUT, **digitalWrite( )** will enable (HIGH) or disable (LOW) the internal pullup on the input pin.
It is recommended to set the **pinMode( )** to INPUT_PULLUP to enable the internal pull-up resistor.
If **pinMode( )** is not set to OUTPUT, and we connect a LED to a pin, then calling **digitalWrite (HIGH)** may make the LED appear dim.
delay (ms)
Pauses the program for the amount of time (in miliseconds) specified by **ms**.

Experiment 1: LED Patterns **19**

More Tweaks

1. Write a sketch to glow LEDs on Application Board one by one from LED1 to LED8. Once LED8 is lit, it should be switched off, and one by one LEDs should be turned off (i.e. LED8 to LED1).

2. Write a sketch to glow odd LEDs (1, 3, 5, 7) on Application board from LED1 to LED8. On return, the LEDs should be put off one by one (7, 5, 3, 1). Make the connections of relevant Arduino pins to Application board LEDs.

3. Write a sketch to glow even LEDs (2, 4, 6, 8) on Application board from LED1 to LED8. On return, the LEDs should be made off one by one (8, 6, 4, 2). Make the connections of relevant Arduino pins to Application board LEDs.

EXPERIMENT TWO

SWITCH BASED LED COUNTER

When I started counting my blessings, my whole life turned around.

- Willie Nelson

Experiment

This Experiment is about developing a binary counter using LEDs. It involves showing numbers on display monitor in decimal and binary format. At the same time, LEDs on the board should glow to represent binary equivalent of the number in question. This should be done for decimal 0 to 255. The process of showing binary representation of LEDs should be controlled through a switch on the board. Once the switch is pressed, the process should start and continue till decimal 255.

Hardware Setup

This Experiment needs an Arduino Uno board and an Application Board. These are shown in Figure 2.1 and 2.2.

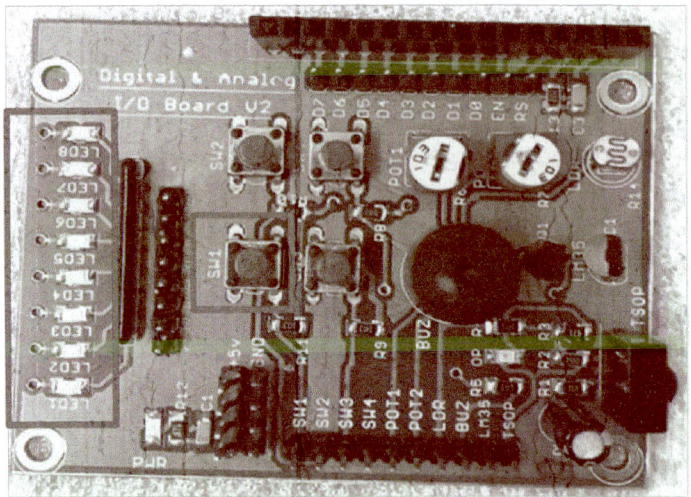

Figure 2.1 Application Board

Experiment 2: Switch based LED Counter **23**

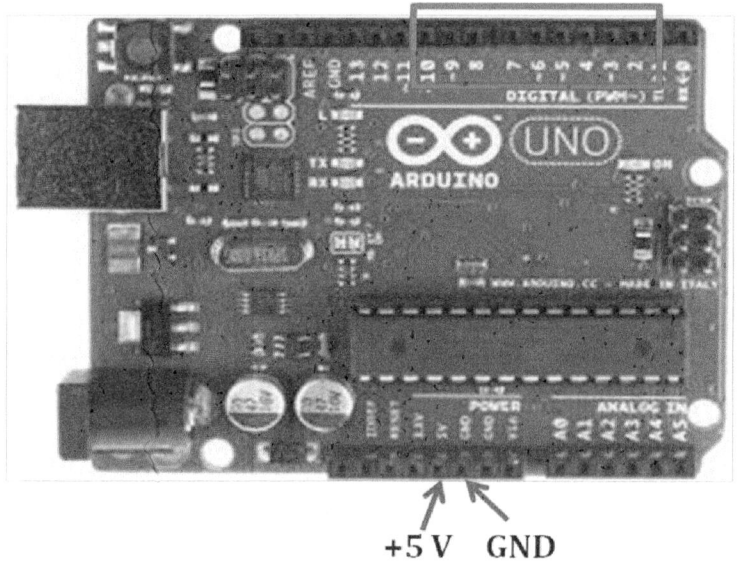

Figure 2.2 Arduino Uno

Pin connections shown in Figure 2.3 should be made.

Arduino Pins	Application Board Pins
+5V	+5V
GND	GND
Digital pin 2	LED1
Digital pin 3	LED2
Digital pin 4	LED3
Digital pin 5	LED4
Digital pin 6	LED5
Digital pin 7	LED6
Digital pin 8	LED7
Digital pin 9	LED8
Sigital pin 10	SW - 1

Figure 2.3 Pin connections

Sketch

```
// Switch controlled binary counter using LEDs
int delay_dur = 2000 ;

// Pins for connecting to LEDs
int ledPin2 = 2 ;
int ledPin3 = 3 ;
int ledPin4 = 4 ;
int ledPin5 = 5 ;
int ledPin6 = 6 ;
int ledPin7 = 7 ;
int ledPin8 = 8 ;
int ledPin9 = 9 ;

int buttonPin = 10 ;  // Pin for Switch 1

// setup function runs once when you press reset or power the board
void setup( )
{
    int i = 0 ;
    int ledPin = 2 ; // Arduino pins 2 to 9 are used

    // Initialize Serial Communication
    Serial.begin ( 9600 ) ;

    for ( i = 0 ; i < 8 ; i++ )
    {
        pinMode ( ledPin, OUTPUT ) ;
        digitalWrite ( ledPin, HIGH ) ; // make LED1 to LED8 OFF
        ledPin = ledPin + 1 ;
    }

    pinMode ( buttonPin, INPUT ) ; // configure button pin as Input

    Serial.println ( "Press Switch-1 to start binary repr. on LEDs " ) ;
    Serial.println ( "Observe equivalent decimal number and binary " ) ;
    Serial.println ( "on the serial monitor" ) ;
}
```

Experiment 2: Switch based LED Counter **25**

```
// the loop function runs over and over again forever
void loop( )
{
    int i = 0 ;
    int number = 0 ;
    int buttonState ;

    buttonstate = digitalRead ( buttonPin ) ;

    if ( buttonState == 0 )
    {
        for ( i = 0 ; i < 256 ; i++ )
        {
            Serial.print ( '\t' ) ;
            Serial.print ( i, DEC ) ; // print decimal number
            Serial.print ( '\t' ) ;
            Serial.println ( i, BIN ) ; // print binary equivalent

            number = i & 1 ; // check if bit 0 is 1 by ANDing with 1

            if ( number )
                digitalWrite ( ledPin9, LOW ) ; // if bit 0 is 1, glow LED8
            else
                digitalWrite ( ledPin9, HIGH ) ; // if bit 0 is 1, do not glow

            number = i & 2 ; // check if bit 1 is 1 by ANDing with 2
            if ( number )
                digitalWrite ( ledPin8, LOW ) ; // if bit 1 is 1, glow LED7
            else
                digitalWrite ( ledPin8, HIGH ) ; // if bit 1 is 0, do not glow

            number = i & 4 ; // check if bit 2 is 1 by ANDing with 4
            if ( number )
                digitalWrite ( ledPin7, LOW ) ; // if bit 2 is 1, glow LED6
            else
                digitalWrite ( ledPin7, HIGH ) ; // if bit 2 is 0, do not glow

            number = i & 8 ; // check if bit 3 is 1 by ANDing with 8
            if ( number )
                digitalWrite ( ledPin6, LOW ) ; // if bit 3 is 1, glow LED5
            else
```

```
            digitalWrite ( ledPin6, HIGH ) ; // if bit 3 is 0, do not glow

        number = i & 16 ; // check if bit 4 is 1 by ANDing with 16
        if ( number )
            digitalWrite ( ledPin5, LOW ) ; // if bit 4 is 1, glow LED4
        else
            digitalWrite ( ledPin5, HIGH ) ; // if bit 4 is 0, do not glow

        number = i & 32 ; // check if bit 5 is 1 by ANDing with 32
        if ( number )
            digitalWrite ( ledPin4, LOW ) ; // if bit 5 is 1, glow LED3
        else
            digitalWrite ( ledPin4, HIGH ) ; // if bit 5 is 0, do not glow

        number = i & 64 ; // check if bit 6 is 1 by ANDing with 64
        if ( number )
            digitalWrite ( ledPin3, LOW ) ; // if bit 6 is 1, glow LED2
        else
            digitalWrite ( ledPin3, HIGH ) ; // if bit 6 is 0, do not glow

        number = i & 128 ; // check if bit 7 is 1 by ANDing with 128
        if ( number )
            digitalWrite ( ledPin2, LOW ) ; // if bit 7 is 1, glow LED1
        else
            digitalWrite ( ledPin2, HIGH ) ; // if bit 7 is 0, do not glow

        delay ( delay_dur ) ; // wait for delay duration
        }
    }
}
```

Result

Once the user presses Switch 1 on the Application board, the display monitor of Arduino IDE shows the decimal numbers from 0 to 255 and their binary equivalents. At the same time, LEDs on the Application board glow, matching the binary representation. For example, if the display monitor shows decimal 5 and binary 101, then LEDs 6 and 8 glow. Similarly, for decimal 18 and 10010, LEDs 4 and 7 glow.

Experiment 2: Switch based LED Counter **27**

The display monitor snapshot is shown in the Figure 2.4.

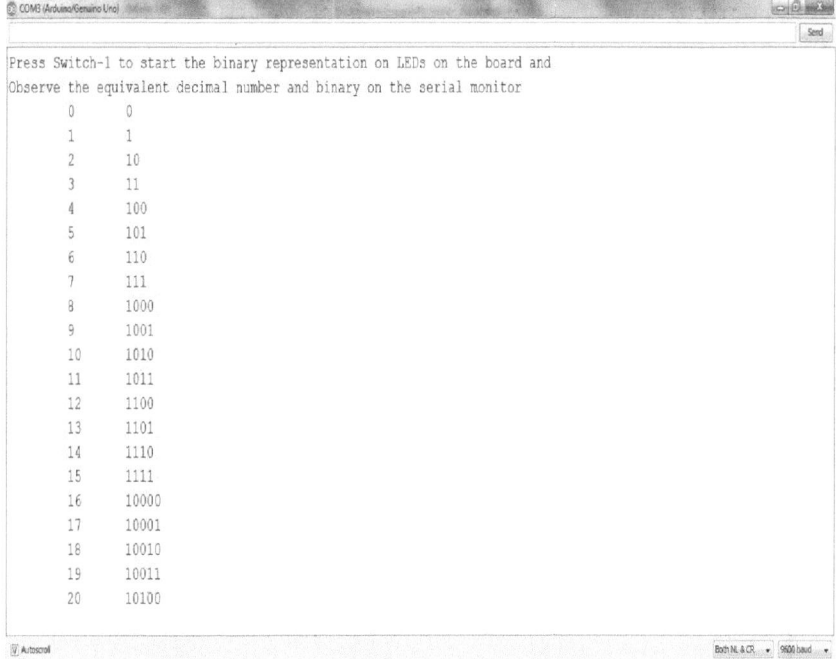

Figure 2.4 Display Monitor Output

Explanation

In the **setup( )** function, pins 2 to 9 are configured as OUTPUT pins using **pinMode( )** function. They are set at HIGH level using **digitalWrite( )** function. The pins are made HIGH so that initially all LEDs are off. Setting HIGH gives 5V at each pin. Since LEDs (1 to 8) on Application board are already connected to +5V, setting HIGH makes them not to glow. This is done using a **for** loop.

The pin 10 of Arduino is configured as INPUT to take input from Switch 1 on the Application board. The variable **buttonPin** is used for pin 10. The **pinMode( )** function is used to configure it.

Serial.begin( ) is used for initialization of serial communication between Arduino IDE's display monitor and the Arduino board. **Serial.Println( )**, is used to show message about pressing Switch 1 to start the binary representation on LEDs and observing the decimal and binary values on display monitor.

In the **loop( )** function, the state of button is read in variable **buttonState** using **digitalRead( )** function. The **digitalRead( )** function reads **buttonPin** value. When Switch 1 is pressed and released the state of **buttonState** becomes '0'.

The **for** loop starts from **i = 0** and goes on till 255. In the **for** loop a call to **Serial.print (i, DEC)** prints value in decimal and **Serial.println (i, BIN)** prints the same value in binary.

i is **AND**ed with 1, 2, 4, 8, 16, 32, 64 and 128 one by one. The variable **number** is used as temporary variable. ANDing with 1 allows checking whether 0th bit is 1. If it is, then LED8 is glown, otherwise not. This is repeated for other bits through the loop.

The loop makes use of the following functions:

digitalWrite (ledpin, LOW) ;
digitalWrite (ledpin, HIGH) ;

When LOW is passed, LED glows, as setting LOW lets the current flow through LED. When HIGH is passed, LED turns off, as setting HIGH does not let the current flow through LED.

Functions Used

Given below is a list of functions that have been used in this Experiment's sketch.

Serial.begin (speed)
It sets the speed in bits per second (baud) for serial data transmission from computer to Arduino board.
speed is baud rate in bits per second.
Serial.print (value)
Prints data to the serial port as human-readable ASCII text.
value represents the value to print.
print( ) returns the number of bytes written (reading that number is optional).
Numbers are printed using an ASCII character for each digit.

Experiment 2: Switch based LED Counter **29**

Floats are printed as ASCII digits, defaulting to two decimal places.

Bytes are sent as a single character.

Characters and strings are sent as is.

Serial.print (value, format)

An optional second parameter specifies the base (format) to use.

format specifies the number base (for integral data types) or number of decimal places (for floating point types).

Permitted values are BIN (binary, or base 2), OCT (octal, or base 8), DEC (decimal, or base 10), HEX (hexadecimal, or base 16).

For floating point numbers, this parameter specifies number of decimal places to print.

Serial.println (value), Serial.println (value, format)

These functions are similar to **Serial.print(value)**, **Serial.print (value, format)**, except that they print the output line by line.

value specifies the value to print.

format specifies the number base (for integral data types) or number of decimal places (for floating point types).

println( ) returns the number of bytes written (reading that number is optional).

digitalRead (pin)

Reads the value from a specified digital pin, either HIGH or LOW.

pin represents the number of the digital pin you want to read (int).

The function returns HIGH or LOW.

If the pin isn't connected to anything, **digitalRead( )** can return either HIGH or LOW (and this can change randomly).

More Tweaks

Enhance the sketch to stop the counter if Switch 2 is pressed for certain duration. Continue counting when Switch 2 is released. Do proper connections to make use of Swtich 2 on the Application Board.

EXPERIMENT THREE

ANALOG I/O: FADE LEDs USING POTENTIOMETER

All that's bright must fade, The brightest still the fleetest; All that's sweet was made But to be lost when sweetest.

- Thomas Moore

Experiment

This Experiment is about controlling the glowing of multiple LEDs using a potentiometer. Initially the LEDs should be fully bright. Then their brightness should reduce in a stepwise fashion, till they are completely off. Again, the LEDs brightness should slowly increase till they become fully bright. This behavior resembles "Fading". The stepwise control should be provided by potentiometer setting.

Hardware Setup

This Experiment needs an Arduino Uno board and an Application Board. These are shown in Figure 3.1 and 3.2.

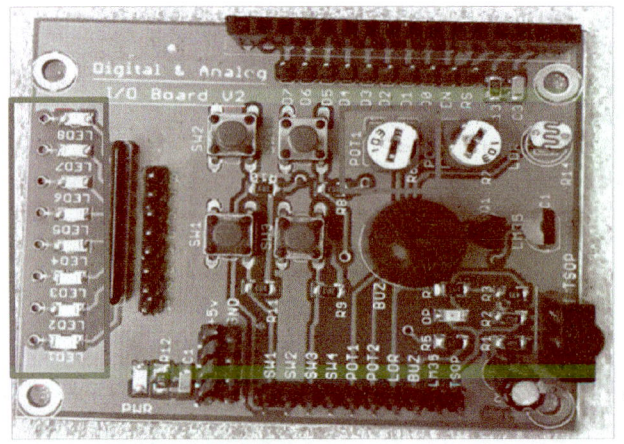

Figure 3.1 Application Board

Experiment 3: Analog I/O: Fade LEDs using Potentiometer **33**

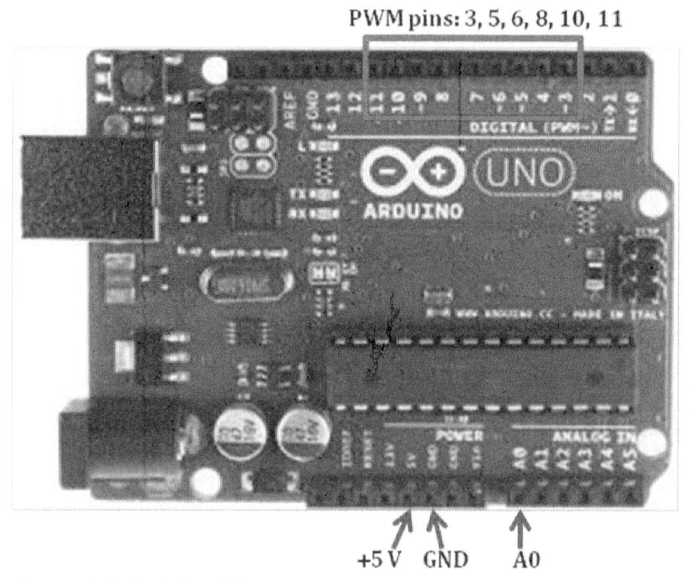

Figure 3.2 Arduino Uno

Pin connections shown in Figure 3.3 should be made.

Arduino Pins	Application Board Pins
+5V	+5V
GND	GND
Digital pin 3	LED1
Digital pin 5	LED2
Digital pin 6	LED3
Digital pin 9	LED4
Digital pin 10	LED5
Digital pin 11	LED6
Analog pin A0	POT1

Figure 3.3 Pin connections

Sketch

```
// Fade  LEDs as per setting of Potentiometer

// how bright the LED is
int brightness = 0 ;
// how many points to fade the LED by
int fadeAmount = 0 ;
// potentiometer value
int sensorValue = 0 ;
// Analog input pin that the potentiometer is attached to
const int analogInPin = A0 ;
int ledArray[ ] = { 3, 5, 6, 9, 10, 11 } ;

void setup( )
{
    // initialize Serial Communication
    Serial.begin( 9600 ) ;

    // read the analog in value
    // read from the pot - 1
    sensorValue = analogRead ( analogInPin ) ;

    // map it to the range of the analog out
    fadeAmount = map ( sensorValue, 0, 1023, 0, 255 ) ;

    Serial.print ( "FadeAmount is: " ) ;
    Serial.println ( fadeAmount ) ;
}

// the loop routine runs over and over again
void loop( )
{
    // set the brightness
    int ledPin = 0 ;
    // size of ledArray: 12 ( i.e. 2 x 6 )
    // size of int: 2, so, len is 6
    int len = sizeof ( ledArray ) / sizeof ( int )  ;

    for ( ledPin = 0 ; ledPin < len ; ledPin++ )
```

Experiment 3: Analog I/O: Fade LEDs using Potentiometer

```
    {
        analogWrite ( ledArray[ ledPin ], brightness );
    }

    // change the brightness for next time through the loop
    brightness = brightness + fadeAmount ;
    Serial.println ( brightness );

    // reverse the direction of the fading at the end of the fade
    if ( brightness <= 0 )
    {
        fadeAmount = -fadeAmount ;
        // avoid negative value
        brightness = 0 ;
    }

    if ( brightness >= 255 )
    {
        fadeAmount = -fadeAmount ;
        // saturate
        brightness = 255 ;
    }

    // wait for some time to see the dimming effect
    delay ( 500 );
}
```

Result

When the sketch is run, the LEDs on the Application board glow fully bright and then after certain delay the brightness reduces. This happens step by step, till they become completely off. Then, once again LEDs start glowing step by step till they become fully bright.

The display monitor shows the fade amount value. The fade amount can be changed by turning potentiometer. The value is set once in setup. It is recommended to keep the potentiometer setting such that **fadeAmount** value is in the range 5 to 50.

Explanation

In the **setup( )** function, the analog pin A0 of Arduino is configured as INPUT to take input from POT 1 on the Application board. The variable **analogInPin** is used for pin A0. The function **analogRead( )** is used to read potentiometer value. The variable **sensorValue** is used for storing this value. The **map( )** function is used to map the values of potentiometer in a range of 0 to 255. The output of this function is stored in the variable **fadeAmount**. **Serial.begin( )** is used for initialization of serial communication between Arduino IDE's display monitor and the Arduino board. **Serial.println( )**, is used to display message about **fadeAmount** value.

In the **loop( )** function, initially LEDs glow to full bright. The function **analogWrite( )** controls the brightness of the LEDs, depending on the value of its second parameter, **brightness**. This function internally uses PWM (Pulse Width Modulation) to control the analog values that are output (written) on the pins. PWM technique is responsible for glowing LEDs at varying brightness. The LEDs glow from full bright to off and vice-versa, based on the following code:

brightness = brightness + fadeAmount ;

To control the direction of fading, **if** statements are used to check whether brightness value is zero (or less) or is 255 (or greater). These statements are shown below.

```
if ( brightness <= 0 )
{
    fadeAmount = -fadeAmount ;
    brightness = 0 ;
}
if ( brightness >= 255 )
{
    fadeAmount = -fadeAmount ;
    brightness = 255 ;
}
```

When these statements are executed, sign of **fadeAmount** reverses.

Experiment 3: Analog I/O: Fade LEDs using Potentiometer **37**

Functions Used

Given below is a list of functions that have been used in this Experiment's sketch.

---

map (value, fromLow, fromHigh, toLow, toHigh)

It does re-mapping of value. A value is mapped as follows:

fromLow is mapped to toLow.

fromHigh is mapped to toHigh.

Values between fromLow to fromHigh are mapped to values between toLow to toHigh.

It does not constrain values to within range because out-of-range values may be needed in a sketch.

The **map( )** function uses integer math so will not generate fractions.

Fractional remainders are truncated, and are not rounded or averaged.

---

analogRead (pin)

Reads the value from the specified analog pin. This value can be pin A0 to pin A5 (6-channel A-D converter).

Returns: 0 to 1023 (integer).

Arduino board contains a 10-bit analog to digital convertor. It maps input voltages between 0 and 5 volts to integer values between 0 and 1023. It has a resolution of .0049 volts (4.9 mV) per unit.

If the analog input pin is not connected to anything, the value returned by **analogRead( )** will fluctuate, based on factors like values of other analog inputs and how close your hand is to the board.

---

analogWrite (pin, value)

Writes an analog value (PWM wave) to a pin.

pin represents the pin to write to.

value is the duty cycle value between 0 and 255.

This function works on pins 3, 5, 6, 9, 10, and 11 (marked with ~ sign on Arduino board).

The pin generates a steady square wave of the specified duty cycle until the next call to **analogWrite( )** or a call to **digitalRead( )** or **digitalWrite( )** on the same pin.

PWM is a technique for getting analog results with digital means. A square wave i.e. a signal switched between on and off is created using digital control. To get varying analog values, change (or modulate), the pulse width.

More Tweaks

1. Modify the sketch to read the POT 1 values in **loop( )** function instead of **setup( )** and to dynamically control the fading of LEDs.
2. Using all the PWM pins write a sketch to generate following pattern:
   - LED1 is off, LED2 is little bright, LED3 still more bright and so on up to LED6 being fully bright.
   - LED6 is off, LED5 is little bright, LED4 still more bright and so on till LED1 being fully bright.
3. Use two potentiometers on the Application board. Connect POT1 to A0 pin and POT2 to A1 pin. Write a sketch to show the output of following on the Serial monitor:
   - Addition of two signals and its result.
   - Subtraction of two signals and its result.
   - Multiplication of two signals and its result.

EXPERIMENT FOUR

USING MILLIS

No matter what your heartache may be, laughing helps you forget it for a few seconds.

- Red Skelton

Experiment

This experiment is about using **millis( )** function. Reading of sensors, mathematical calculations or pin manipulations cannot go on during the execution of **delay( )** function. It brings most other activity to halt. The function **millis( )** overcomes these drawbacks. This experiment shows how to use **millis( )** to create a pattern of LEDs.

Hardware Setup

This Experiment needs an Arduino Uno board and an Application Board. These are shown in Figure 4.1 and 4.2.

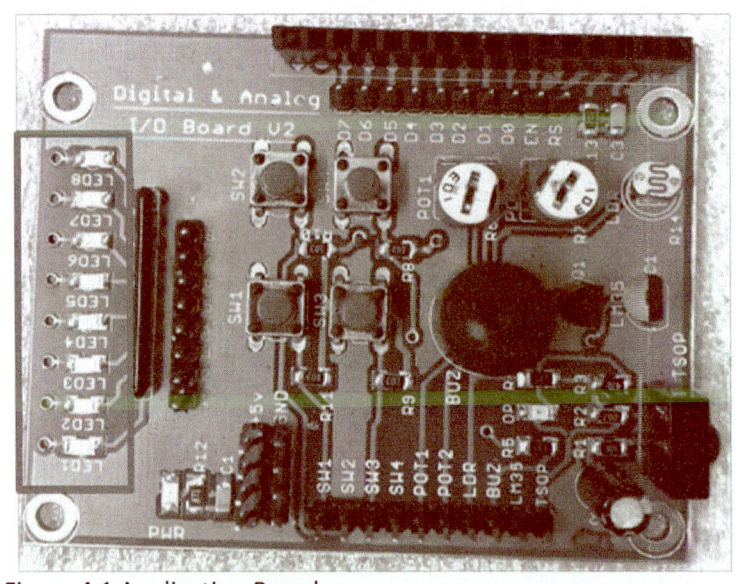

Figure 4.1 Application Board

Experiment 4: Using Millis   **41**

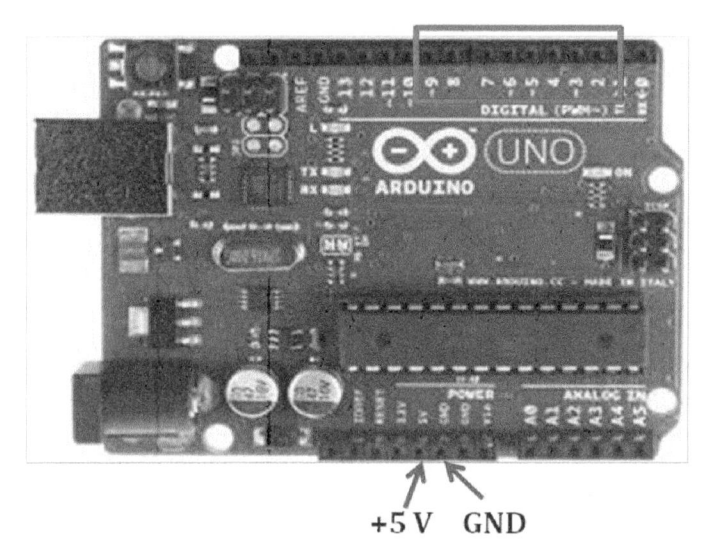

Figure 4.2 Arduino Uno

Pin connections shown in Figure 4.3 should be made.

Arduino Pins	Application Board Pins
+5V	+5V
GND	GND
Digital pin 2	LED1
Digital pin 3	LED2
Digital pin 4	LED3
Digital pin 5	LED4
Digital pin 6	LED5
Digital pin 7	LED6
Digital pin 8	LED7
Digital pin 9	LED8

Figure 4.3 Pin connections

Sketch

```
// Using millis( ) make LED pattern

// store last time LED was updated
unsigned long previousMillis = 0 ;

// constants won't change
// interval at which to blink (milliseconds)
const long interval = 1000 ;

int count = 0 ;
// 1: direction is from LED1 to LED8
// 0: direction is from LED8 to LED1
byte dir = 1 ;

void makeLEDs_Off( )
{
    for ( int ledPin = 2 ; ledPin <= 9 ; ledPin++ )
    {
        // make LED1 to LED8 off (not glow)
        digitalWrite ( ledPin, HIGH ) ;
    }
}

void setup( )
{
    Serial.begin ( 9600 ) ;
    for ( int ledPin = 2 ; ledPin <= 9 ; ledPin++ )
    {
        // configure pins as OUTPUT
        pinMode ( ledPin, OUTPUT ) ;
        // make LED1 to LED8  off ( not glow )
        digitalWrite ( ledPin, HIGH ) ;
    }
}

void loop( )
{
```

Experiment 4: Using Millis

```
        unsigned long currentMillis = millis( ) ;

    if ( currentMillis - previousMillis >= interval )
    {
        // save the last time you blinked the LED
        previousMillis = currentMillis ;

        int pin ;
        if ( dir == 1 )
        {
            count ++ ;
            pin = count + 1 ;
            if ( pin > 1 && pin < 10 )
            digitalWrite ( pin , LOW ) ;
        }

        if ( count > 9 )
        {
            // Reverse the direction
            dir = !dir ;
            // make all LEDs off
            makeLEDs_Off( ) ;
        }

        if ( dir == 0 )
        {
            pin = count ;
            if ( pin > 1 && pin < 10 )
                digitalWrite ( pin , LOW ) ;
            count -- ;
        }

        if ( count == 0 )
        {
            // reverse the direction
            dir = !dir ;
            // make all LEDs off
            makeLEDs_Off( ) ;
        }
    }
}
```

Result

- When the sketch is executed, the LEDs on the Application board glow one by one, from LED1 to LED8 (forward direction).
- Then all the LEDs are off for certain interval.
- Then LEDs glow one by one, from LED8 to LED1 (reverse direction).
- Then all the LEDs are off.
- Once again, pattern starts in forward direction, then in reverse direction, and continues to repeat as long as the board is on.

Explanation

In the **setup( )** function, the Arduino pins 2 to 9 are configured as OUTPUT and these pins are made HIGH so that initially all LEDs are off. As LEDs on the Application board are connected to +5V, setting these pins to HIGH makes them off, as current does not flow. This is done by calling **makeLEDs_Off( )** function.

The global variables defined in the sketch are **previousMillis, dir, interval** and **count**. The **previousMillis** and **count** are initialized to 0. The **dir** variable is initialized to 1 and **interval** to 1000 (milliseconds).

In the **loop( )** function, the **previousMillis** is used to store the previous value of the **currentMillis**. The **currentMillis** variable stores current time. When the difference between **currentMillis** and **previousMillis** is more than a constant interval, further code executes.

The **count** variable is used as counter to glow LEDs one by one in forward and reverse direction. The LEDs glow at constant interval duration. **count** is used to calculate the pin value, so that corresponding LED glows correctly.

When **count** becomes greater than 9, the direction is reversed and all the LEDs are made off using **makeLEDs_Off( )** function. This is done using following code:

```
if ( count > 9 )
{
    dir = ! dir ;
    makeLEDs_Off( ) ;
}
```

Experiment 4: Using Millis

When count becomes 0, the direction is reversed and all the LEDs are made off using **makeLEDs_Off( )** function. This is done using following code:

```
if ( count == 0 )
{
    dir = ! dir ;
    makeLEDs_Off( ) ;
}
```

The variable **dir** is used to control LEDs glow direction from LED1 to LED8 and vice-versa. It is initialized to 1 for glowing LEDs from LED1 to LED8. Its value is made 0 in the reverse direction. The following code snippets shows working of **dir**:

```
if ( dir == 1 )
{
    count ++ ;
    pin = count + 1 ;
    if ( pin > 1 && pin < 10 )
        digitalWrite ( pin , LOW ) ;
}
if ( dir == 0 )
{
    pin = count ;
    if ( pin > 1 && pin < 10 )
        digitalWrite ( pin , LOW ) ;
    count -- ;
}
```

The **if (pin > 1 && pin < 10)** statement is used to ensure that pins between 2 and 9 alone are updated via **digitalWrite( )** while other pins are not.

Function Used

Given below is a function that has been used in this Experiment's sketch.

---
millis( )

It returns the number of milliseconds since the Arduino board began running the current program.

This number overflows (is reset to zero) after approximately 50 days.

Data type to be used should be **unsigned long**.

Note:

- Logic errors may occur if a programmer tries to do arithmetic with smaller data types such as integer.
- Using **signed long** may encounter errors as its maximum value is half that of **unsigned long**.

More Tweaks

1. Write a sketch to blink LED1 of Application board while reading a Switch 1 button press.
2. Demonstrate by developing a sketch, that **delay( )** cannot do the same job.

EXPERIMENT FIVE

REMOTE CONTROL BASED MELODY PLAYER

As a melody instrument player, it's all about getting from one note to the next, and those intervals and how you navigate your way through these vertical structures of chords. You realize that everything's moving forward, and it's all linear.

- David Sanborn

Experiment

This experiment is about developing a Remote Control controlled melody player. As you press different keys (like 1, 2, 3 etc.) on the Remote Control, you should hear a different melody for each key press. This involves interaction of Remote Control with IR (infra red) detector and the Buzzer for playing melodies.

Hardware Setup

This Experiment needs an Arduino Uno board and an Application Board. These are shown in Figure 5.1 and 5.2.

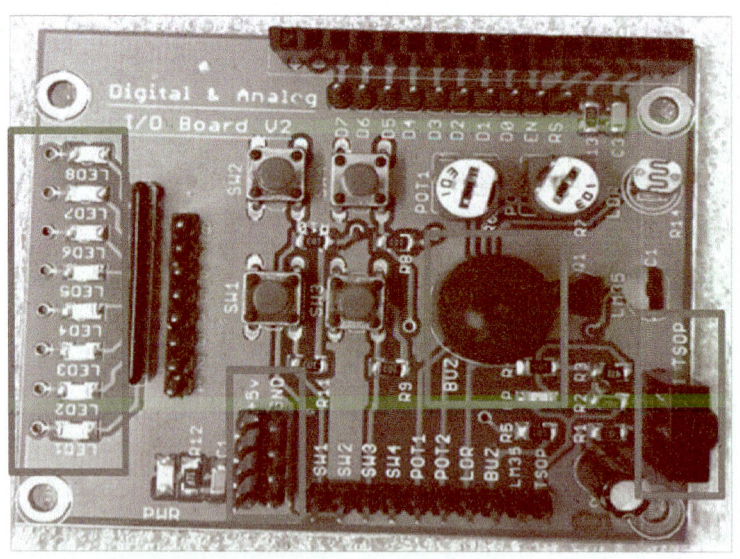

Figure 5.1 Application Board

Experiment 5: Remote Control based Melody Player **49**

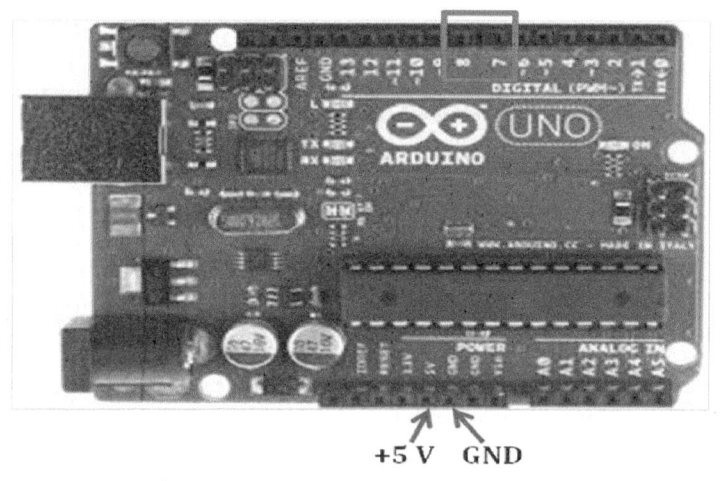

Figure 5.2 Arduino Uno

Pin connections shown in Figure 5.3 should be made.

Arduino Pins	Application Board Pins
+5V	+5V
GND	GND
Digital pin 7	BUZ
Digital pin 8	TSOP

Figure 5.3 Pin connections

The Remote Control to be used for this experiment is shown in Figure 5.4. It's a remote control for the Cisco Set-top-box and used by one of the service provider UCN.

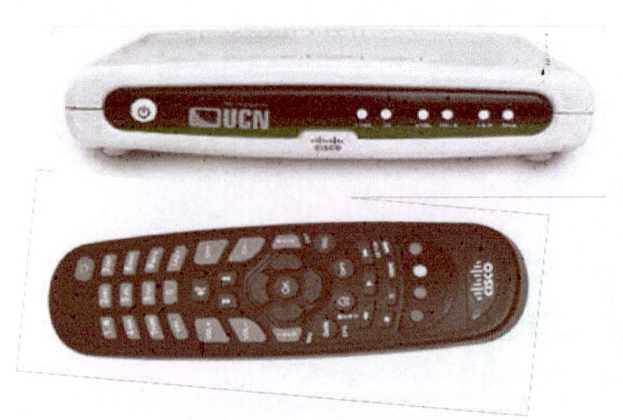

Figure 5.4 Remote Control (used with UCN/ Cisco Set-top-box)

Sketch

// Remote Controlled based sound melody player

#include "pitches.h"

// notes in the melody
int melody1[ ] = { NOTE_C4, NOTE_G3, NOTE_G3, NOTE_A3, NOTE_G3,
                0, NOTE_B3, NOTE_C4 } ;
int melody2[ ] = { NOTE_F3, NOTE_G3, NOTE_C3, NOTE_A3, NOTE_F4,
                0, NOTE_B3, NOTE_C4 } ;
int melody3[ ] = { NOTE_F3, NOTE_G3, NOTE_C3, NOTE_D3, NOTE_F4,
                0, NOTE_E3, NOTE_D4 } ;
int melody4[ ] = { NOTE_F1, NOTE_G3, NOTE_C3, NOTE_B3, NOTE_F4,
                0, NOTE_G3, NOTE_C4 } ;
int melody5[ ] = { NOTE_F3, NOTE_G3, NOTE_C3, NOTE_A3, NOTE_F4,
                0, NOTE_A3, NOTE_E4 } ;

// note durations: 4 = quarter note, 8 = eighth note, etc.:
int noteDurations1[ ] = { 4, 8, 8, 4, 4, 4, 4, 4 } ;
int noteDurations2[ ] = { 8, 4, 8, 4, 8, 2, 4, 4 } ;
int noteDurations3[ ] = { 8, 4, 8, 4, 8, 2, 2, 4 } ;
int noteDurations4[ ] = { 8, 4, 2, 4, 8, 2, 16, 4 } ;
int noteDurations5[ ] = { 16, 2, 8, 4, 8, 4, 4, 4 } ;

// buz pin

Experiment 5: Remote Control based Melody Player

```
int tonePin = 7 ;

// infrared pin
int irPin = 8 ;

void setup( )
{
    pinMode ( irPin, INPUT ) ;
    Serial.begin ( 9600 ) ;

    Serial.println ( "Remote Controlled melody player" ) ;
    Serial.println ( "Press a key from 1 to 5 to play a melody" ) ;
}

// Step 1: Read the duration (of pulses) of key pressed using micros( )
// on the Remote Control and store in an array
// Step 2: Find out the exact key pressed based on the code
void loop( )
{
    int bits_len = 24 ;
    unsigned int arr[ bits_len ] ;
    unsigned long val = 0 ;
    unsigned long startTime, endTime ;

    // loop till any key on remote is not pressed
    // when key is pressed the value is LOW
    while ( digitalRead ( irPin ) == HIGH )
        ;

    // loop to receive 24 bits of key press on remote control
    for ( int i = 0 ; i < bits_len ; i++ )
    {
        // loop till a key is pressed
        while ( digitalRead ( irPin ) == LOW )
            ;

        // once a key is pressed note the start time
        startTime = micros( ) ;

        // loop till key is released
        while ( digitalRead ( irPin ) == HIGH )
```

```
        ;

    // after key is released note the end time
    endTime = micros( ) ;

    // store the difference in the time interval
    arr[ i ] = endTime - startTime ;
}

for ( int i = 0 ; i < bits_len ; i++ )
{
    // if the time interval more than 1000 microseconds
    if ( arr[ i ] > 1000 )
    {
        // binary to decimal conversion
        // 1 << i is nothing but 2 raised to the power of i
        val = val + ( 1l << i ) ;
    }
}

switch ( val )
{
    // Key 1, channel 1
    case 0x25FA03 :
        erial.println ( "Playing melody-1" ) ;
        play_melody ( melody1, noteDurations1 ) ;
        break ;

    // Key 2, channel 2
    case 0x27FA03 :
        Serial.println ( "Playing melody-2" ) ;
        play_melody ( melody2, noteDurations2 ) ;
        break ;

    // Key 3, channel 3
    case 0x99FA03 :
        Serial.println ( "Playing melody-3" ) ;
        play_melody ( melody3, noteDurations3 ) ;
        break ;

    // Key 4, channel 4
```

Experiment 5: Remote Control based Melody Player

```
            case 0x1DFA03 :
                Serial.println ( "Playing melody-4" ) ;
                play_melody ( melody4, noteDurations4 ) ;
                break ;

            // Key 5, channel 5
            case 0x1FFA03 :
                Serial.println ( "Playing melody-5" ) ;
                play_melody ( melody5, noteDurations5 ) ;
                break ;

            case 0x91FA03 :
                Serial.println ( "Key 6" ) ;
                delay ( 1000 ) ;
                break ;

            case 0x15FA03 :
                Serial.println ( "Key 7") ;
                delay ( 1000 ) ;
                break ;

            case 0x17FA03 :
                Serial.println ( "Key 8" ) ;
                delay ( 1000 ) ;
                break ;

            case 0x89FA03 :
                Serial.println ( "Key 9" ) ;
                delay ( 1000 ) ;
                break ;

            default :
                Serial.println ( "Press any key from 1 to 9" ) ;
        }
}
void play_melody ( int melody[ ], int noteDurations[ ] )
{
    for ( int thisNote = 0 ; thisNote < 8 ; thisNote++ )
    {
```

```
        // to calculate the note duration, take one second
        // divided by the note type
        // i.e. quarter note = 1000 / 4, eighth note = 1000 / 8, etc.

        int noteDuration = 1000 / noteDurations[ thisNote ] ;
        tone ( tonePin, melody[ thisNote ], noteDuration ) ;

        // to distinguish the notes, set a minimum time between them.
        // the note's duration + 30% work well:
        int pauseBetweenNotes = noteDuration * 1.30 ;
        delay ( pauseBetweenNotes ) ;
        // stop the tone playing
        noTone ( tonePin ) ;
    }
}
```

Result

- When the sketch is run, a message is displayed saying "Press a key from 1 to 5 to play a melody".

- On pressing key 1 on the Remote Control you should hear a melody. The message is also shown in the display monitor that melody-1 is playing.

- On repeating the above steps for keys 2 to 5, you should hear different melodies. The message is also shown in the display monitor that a particular melody is playing.

- If key 6 to 9 is pressed, a message that a key is pressed is displayed. You can enhance the sketch to play other melodies in such cases.

- If any other key is pressed a message mentioning "Press a key between 1 and 9" is displayed.

Explanation

The "pitches.h" header file is available in the Arduino IDE installed folder "C:\Program Files (x86)\Arduino\examples\02.Digital\toneMelody".

Experiment 5: Remote Control based Melody Player

Copy "pitches.h" to the directory where the sketch file of experiment is created.

In the **setup( )** function, the Arduino pin 7 is configured as INPUT. The variable used for this pin is **irPin**. The **Serial.begin( )** function is used to initialize the serial communication and **Serial.println( )** to display messages.

The global variables **melody1[ ]**, **melody2[ ]**, **melody3[ ]**, **melody4[ ]**, **melody5[ ]** are used to store the melodies that are to be played. Each melody is made up of 8 notes. The variables **noteDurations1[ ]**, **noteDurations2[ ]**, etc. are used to store the durations for which the notes are to be played. The variable **tonePin** is used for connection with buzzer (BUZ pin) and the variable **irPin** is used for connection with IR detector (TSOP pin).

The **loop( )** function is broadly divided into two steps:

(a) Reading the duration (of pulses) of key pressed on the Remote Control using **micros( )** function and storing this in an array. The pulses are represented in binary format in the array.

(b) Finding the exact key pressed, based on the pulses that are received on pressing a key on the Remote Control. Here binary to decimal conversion is done.

The **bits_len** variable is set to 24. This value is based on the experimentation done with the Cisco Remote Control.

The **loop( )** waits till the value read is HIGH. This is done using following code:

```
while ( digitalRead ( irPin ) == HIGH )
    ;
```

When a key is pressed, the pulse value is 0. The time is measured using **micros( )** function after key is pressed and is assigned to variable **startTime**. Time is again measured when key is released and stored in the variable **endTime**. The difference in the two times is stored in **arr[ ]**.

The **digitalRead( )** function is used to read value of **irPin**. This is done using the following code:

```
for ( int i = 0 ; i < bits_len ; i++ )
{
```

```
    while ( digitalRead ( irPin ) == LOW )
        ;
    startTime = micros( ) ;

    while ( digitalRead ( irPin ) == HIGH )
        ;
    endTime = micros( ) ;

    arr[ i ] = endTime - startTime ;
}
```

If the value stored in **arr[ ]** **is** greater than 1000 then its decimal equivalent is obtained using the following code:

```
for ( int i = 0 ; i < bits_len ; i++ )
{
    if ( arr[ i ] > 1000 )
    {
        val = val + ( 1l << i ) ;
    }
}
```

Finally, a **switch-case** is used for matching unique ID of each of the keys on the Remote Control. The function **play_melody( )** is called from various cases to play different melodies.

Function Used

The important function used in this Experiment's sketch is given below.

---
micros( )

- Returns the number of microseconds since the Arduino board began running the current program.
- This number will overflow (go back to zero) after approximately 70 minutes.
- **unsigned long** should be used to store the value returned by this function.

Experiment 5: Remote Control based Melody Player

More Tweaks

1. Enhance the sketch to play melodies for key press 6 to 9.
2. Develop a new sketch to handle different remote controls. The above sketch can be debugged and modified to find out how many bits a remote is using. The use of **pulseIn( )** can be explored to understand the protocol used by TV remote. One such example is SIRC (Serial Infra-Red Control) protocol.

EXPERIMENT SIX

USING EEPROM TO CONTROL DEVICES

The function of memory is not only to preserve, but also to throw away. If you remembered everything from your entire life, you would be sick.

- Umberto Eco

Experiment

EEPROM is the memory where values are preserved when power supply to the Arduino Uno board is turned off. This Experiment consists of two sketches. In the first sketch EEPROM library is used to store objects to EEPROM. In the second sketch the objects stored by first sketch are read back. The read objects are then used to control devices (e.g. LEDs, Buzzer). The objects read from EEPROM are also shown on the Display monitor.

Hardware Setup

This Experiment needs an Arduino Uno board and an Application Board. These are shown in Figure 6.1 and 6.2.

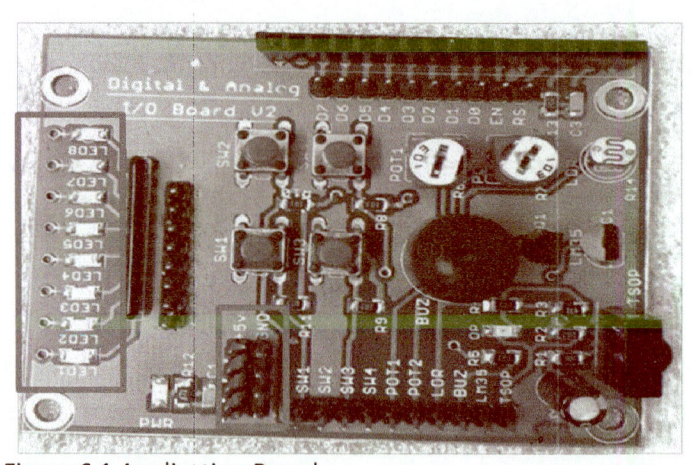

Figure 6.1 Application Board

Experiment 6: Using EEPROM to Control Devices

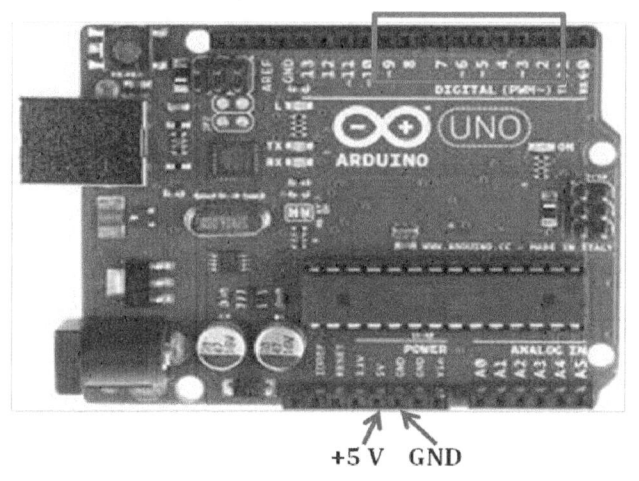

Figure 6.2 Arduino Uno

Pin connections shown in Figure 6.3 should be made.

Arduino Pins	Application Board Pins
+5V	+5V
GND	GND
Digital pin 2	LED1
Digital pin 3	LED2
Digital pin 4	LED3
Digital pin 5	LED4
Digital pin 6	LED5
Digital pin 7	LED6
Digital pin 8	LED7
Digital pin 9	LED8

Figure 6.3 Pin connections

Sketches

ledStruct.h

```
struct LEDData
{
    int ledno ;
    char name[ 8 ] ;
} ;
```

Sketch 1

```
// Writes object to EEPROM
#include "ledStruct.h"
#include <EEPROM.h>

// current address in the EEPROM
// i.e. which byte we're going to write to next
int addr = 0 ;

void setup( )
{
    Serial.begin ( 9600 ) ;
    put_to_EEPROM( ) ;
}

void put_to_EEPROM( )
{
    LEDData data[ 9 ] = {
                        { 0, "OFF" },
                        { 1, "LED-1" },
                        { 2, "LED-2" },
                        { 3, "LED-3" },
                        { 4, "LED-4" },
                        { 5, "LED-5" },
                        { 6, "LED-6" },
                        { 7, "LED-7" },
                        { 8, "LED-8" }
                        } ;
```

Experiment 6: Using EEPROM to Control Devices 63

```
        int address = 0 ;
        for ( int i = 0 ; i <= 8 ; i++ )
        {
            // writes data at 0, 1, 2...8
            EEPROM.put ( address, data[ i ] ) ;
            // write after sizeof struct
            address = address + sizeof ( struct LEDData ) ;
            delay ( 100 ) ;
        }
    }

    void loop( )
    {
        // nothing in the loop
        // write data once to EEPROM in setup( ) function
    }
```

Sketch 2

```
// Reads object from EEPROM
#include "ledStruct.h"
#include <EEPROM.h>

// the current address in EEPROM
int addr = 0 ;
const int delay_dur = 1000 ;

void setup( )
{
    Serial.begin ( 9600 ) ;

    for ( int ledPin = 2 ; ledPin <= 9 ; ledPin++ )
    {
        // configure pins as OUTPUT
        pinMode ( ledPin,OUTPUT ) ;
        // make LED1 to LED8 off (not glow)
        digitalWrite ( ledPin, HIGH ) ;
    }
}
```

```
void make_LEDsOff( )
{
    for ( int ledPin = 2 ; ledPin <= 9 ; ledPin++ )
    {
        // make LED1 to LED8 OFF ( not glow )
        digitalWrite ( ledPin, HIGH ) ;
    }
}

void loop( )
{
    // object of struct LEDData
    LEDData ledData ;
    // calculate index i based on address and sizeof struct LEDData
    int i = addr / sizeof ( struct LEDData ) ;
    EEPROM.get ( addr, ledData ) ;

    Serial.print ( ledData.ledno ) ;
    Serial.print ( "\t" ) ;
    Serial.println ( ledData.name ) ;
    if ( i == 0 )
    {
        make_LEDsOff( ) ;
        delay ( delay_dur ) ;
    }
    else
    {
        // glow LEDs one by one
        // add 1 to get pin 2 to 9
        digitalWrite ( ledData.ledno + 1, LOW ) ;
        delay ( delay_dur ) ;
    }

    // increment the address by the size of structure LEDData
    addr = addr + sizeof ( struct LEDData ) ;
    if ( addr > ( 8 * sizeof ( struct LEDData ) ) )
    {
        // restart after addr is above 8 objects
        addr = 0 ;
    }
}
```

Experiment 6: Using EEPROM to Control Devices

Result

- When Sketch 1 is executed, it stores object values consisting of pairs of LED number, and its name. For example 1, "LED-1". Sketch 1 also stores object with number 0 and corresponding string "OFF".
- Power off the Arduino board after Sketch 1 is executed.
- When Sketch 2 is executed, it reads the stored object values and glows the LEDs as per the values read from EEPROM. The read values are also displayed on the Display monitor.

Explanation

Sketch 1 includes a header file "EEPROM.h" which supports reading / writing from / to EEPROM. A structure **LEDData** consisting of fields **ledno, name[ ]** is declared as follows in the file ledStruct.h:

```
struct LEDData
{
    int ledno ;
    char name[ 8 ] ;
};
```

In the **setup( )** function, **Serial.begin( )** is used to initialize the serial communication. A function **put_to_EEPROM( )** writes the data to EEPROM. It creates **data[ ]**, an array of **LEDData** structures. This array is initialized to different LED numbers and their names.

The variable **address** is initialized to 0. In the **for** loop, **EEPROM.put( )** function of EEPROM library is used to write **data[ ]** values to EEPROM. After writing each record, the address where next pair of values is to be written is incremented by **sizeof (struct LEDData)** bytes. The following code shows this:

```
for ( int i = 0 ; i <= 8 ; i++ )
{
    EEPROM.put ( address, data[ i ] ) ;
    address = address + sizeof ( struct LEDData ) ;
    delay ( 100 ) ;
```

}

There is no code in the **loop( )** function as writing to EEPROM should be done only once.

Note that the function **EEPROM.put( )** uses **EEPROM.update( )** to perform the write, so it does not rewrite a value if it hasn't changed since the last write.

Sketch 2 includes a header file "EEPROM.h" which supports reading/writing from/to EEPROM. The header file "ledStruct.h" is also included in this sketch.

The variable **addr** is initialized to 0 and it holds the current address of EEPROM location from where records are to be read. The **delay_dur** variable is initialized to 1000 ms.

In the **setup( )** function, **Serial.begin( )** is used to initialized for serial communication. The pins used for connecting to LEDs are configured as OUTPUT. It is set to HIGH to ensure that initially all LEDs are off.

In the **loop( )** function, object **ledData** is created for **struct LEDData**. The index **i** is calculated using **addr** and size of structure as follows:

int i = addr / sizeof (struct LEDData) ;

EEPROM.get( ) , is used to read the object values stored in EEPROM in Sketch1. The led number and name read into the object are then displayed on the Display monitor. The code that achieves this is as follows:

EEPROM.get (addr, ledData) ;
Serial.print (ledData.ledno) ;
Serial.print ("\t") ;
Serial.println (ledData.name) ;

When the index **i** is 0, all the LEDs are made off using the function **make_LEDsOff( )**. When index **i** is more than 0 then LEDs glow one by from LED1 to LED8. Arduino pins 2 to 9 are used to control LED1 to LED8 on the application board, hence 1 is added to **ledData.ledno**. The code that achieves this is given below.

if (i == 0)
{

Experiment 6: Using EEPROM to Control Devices

```
        make_LEDsOff( ) ;
        delay ( delay_dur ) ;
    }
    else
    {
        digitalWrite ( ledData.ledno + 1 , LOW ) ;
        delay ( delay_dur ) ;
    }
```

The address is incremented by the size of structure **LEDData**. When the address is more than 8 times the size of structure, **addr** is reset to 0. 8 is used because Sketch 1 defines array of structure of size 9. The code that achieves this is given below.

```
addr = addr + sizeof ( struct LEDData ) ;
if ( addr > ( 8 * sizeof ( struct LEDData ) ) )
{
    addr = 0 ;
}
```

Functions Used

Given below is a list of functions that have been used in this Experiment's sketches.

EEPROM.get (address, data)
Read any data type or object from the EEPROM.
address: the location to read from, starting from 0 (int).
data: the data to read, can be a primitive type (e.g. int, float) or a custom struct.
Return: A reference to the data passed in.
EEPROM.put (address, data)
Write any data type or object to EEPROM.
address: the location to write to, starting from 0 (int).
data: the data to read. It can be a primitive type (e.g. int, float), or a

> custom struct.
>
> Return: A reference to the data passed as parameter.

More Tweaks

- Develop two sketches. The first sketch should store multiple melodies to the EEPROM. The second sketch should read these stored melodies and play it to the buzzer on the application board in a sequence.
- Enhance the above sketch to play melodies in random order.
- Explore EEPROM methods **EEPROM.write( )** and **EEPROM.read( )** and develop similar sketches.

CHAPTER SEVEN

MOTOR SPEED CONTROL

It's hard to regulate the speed at which you can achieve something creative and emotional.

- Carol Kane

Experiment

This experiment is about linear speed control of a DC motor using a potentiometer. This should be achieved by using the PWM (Pulse Width Modulation) technique.

Hardware Setup

This Experiment needs an Arduino Uno board, Application Board, Motor Driver board and DC motor. These are shown in Figures 7.1, 7.2 and 7.3.

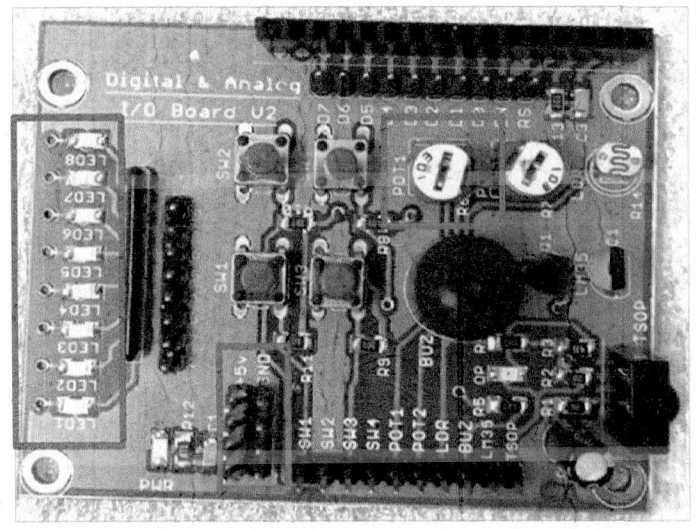

Figure 7.1 Application Board

Experiment 7: Motor Speed Control **71**

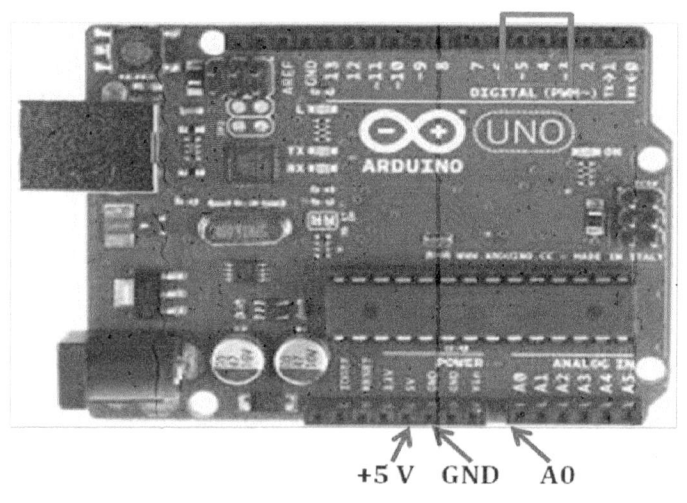

Figure 7.2 Arduino Uno

Figure 7.3 Motor Driver and DC Motor

The pin connections shown in Figure 7.4 should be made.

Arduino Pins	Application Board Pins
+5V	+5V
GND	GND
Analog pin A0	POT 1

Arduino Pins	Motor Driver Board Pins
Vin	+12V
Digital pin 4	IN 1
Digital pin 5	IN 2

Application Board Pins	Motor Driver Board Pins
+5V	+5V
GND	GND

Motor Driver Board Pins	DC Motor
LEFT (+)	Red wire (Terminal 1)
LEFT (-)	Black wire (Terminal 2)

Figure 7.4 Pin connections

Sketch

```
// Speed Control of DC Motor via Potentiometer

int potPin = A0 ;
// PWM pin
// Pin 5 and 4 to provide voltage to the motor
int pwmPin = 5 ;
int digPin = 4 ;

void setup( )
{
```

Experiment 7: Motor Speed Control **73**

```
    Serial.begin ( 9600 ) ;
    Serial.println ( "Motor control via potentiometer" ) ;
    // PWM pin
    pinMode ( pwmPin, OUTPUT ) ;
    // DC Motor, pwm pin intially set to LOW
    digitalWrite ( pwmPin, LOW ) ;
    pinMode ( digPin, OUTPUT ) ;
    // DC motor LOW
    digitalWrite ( digPin, LOW ) ;
}

void loop( )
{
    // Read POT 1 value
    int val = analogRead ( potPin ) ;
    // Map the values in the range 0-255
    int potValue = map ( val, 0, 1023, 0, 255 ) ;
    Serial.println ( potValue ) ;

    setMotorSpeed ( potValue ) ;
}

void setMotorSpeed ( int pwmVal )
{
    // writes as per POT 1 value
    analogWrite ( pwmPin , pwmVal ) ;
    // set to LOW
    digitalWrite ( digPin , LOW ) ;
}
```

Result

- When the Sketch is executed DC motor rotates at a speed depending on the position of the POT 1.

- On rotating POT 1 in either direction, the speed will change. The speed will either decrease or increase depending on the direction of rotation.

Explanation

To change speed of the DC motor rotate the potentiometer 1 in either direction after sketch is uploaded to the Arduino board.

The sketch starts with the declaration of global variables. The variable **potPin** is for reading potentiometer values. The variables **pwmPin** and **digPin** are used for controlling speed of the DC motor

In the **setup( )** function, the serial communication is initialized using **Serial.begin( )**. The **pwmPin** and **digPin** are configured as OUTPUT. Both the pins are set to LOW via **digitalWrite( )**.

In the **loop( )** function, the POT 1 values are read using **analogRead( )**. The values are mapped in the range 0 to 255 via the **map( )** function. The potentiometer values are shown on the display monitor. The motor speed is set using **setMotorSpeed( )** which takes potentiometer values. The **analogWrite( )** method writes value to **pwmPin** which effectively controls the speed of the motor. The following code achieves this:

```
int val = analogRead ( potPin ) ;
int potValue = map ( val, 0, 1023, 0, 255 ) ;
Serial.println ( potValue ) ;
setMotorSpeed ( potValue ) ;

void setMotorSpeed ( int pwmVal )
{
    analogWrite ( pwmPin , pwmVal ) ;
    digitalWrite ( digPin , LOW ) ;
}
```

Functions Used

The functions used in this sketch are already covered in the previous experiments.

Experiment 7: Motor Speed Control

More Tweaks

1. Develop a sketch to rotate the DC motor in clockwise direction for a fixed duration and then the motor should stop. Again the motor should rotate but in anticlockwise direction, for a fixed duration and then stop.
2. Enhance the above sketch to use potentiometer to control the speed in either direction.

CHAPTER EIGHT

ACCELEROMETER BASED ROTATION CONTROL

I shall now recall to mind that the motion of the heavenly bodies is circular, since the motion appropriate to a sphere is rotation in a circle.

- *Nicolaus Copernicus*

Experiment

This Experiment is about using Accelerometer / Gyroscope sensor to control the direction of rotation of a DC motor as per the change of orientation of the sensor. The single sensor contains both Accelerometer as well as Gyroscope. Accelerometer measures acceleration on one, two or three axes, whereas, Gyroscope measures rate of rotation around a particular axis.

Hardware Setup

This Experiment needs an Arduino Uno board, Application board, Motor Driver board, DC motor and Accelerometer / Gyro MPU-6050 board. These are shown in the Figures 8.1, 8.2, 8.3, 8.4 and 8.5.

Figure 8.1 Application Board

Experiment 8: Accelerometer based Rotation Control　　**79**

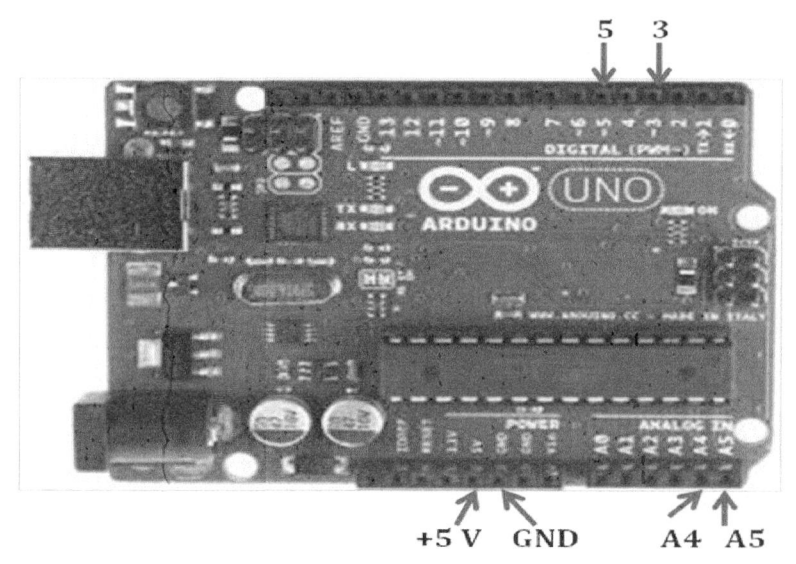

Figure 8.2 Arduino Uno

Motor Driver

DC Motor

Figure 8.3 Motor Driver Figure 8.4 DC Motor

Figure 8.5 MPU-6050 Accelerometer/Gyro (2 different different makes)

The pin connections shown in Figure 8.6 should be made. The Application board is mainly used to provide +5V and GND pins as part of the +5V and GND rails.

Arduino Pins	Application Board Pins
+5V	+5V
GND	GND

Application Board Pins	MPU-6050 Board Pins
+5V	VCC (+5V)
GND	GND

Arduino Pins	Motor Driver Board Pins
Vin	+12 V
Digital pin 3	IN 1
Digital pin 5	IN 2

Arduino Pins	MPU-6050 Board Pins
Digital pin 2	INT
Analog A4 pin	SDA
Analog A5 pin	SCL

Experiment 8: Accelerometer based Rotation Control **81**

Application Board Pins	Motor Driver Board Pins
+5V GND	+5V GND

Motor Driver Board Pins	DC Motor
LEFT (+) LEFT (-)	Red wire (Terminal 1) Black wire (Terminal 2)

Figure 8.6 Pin connections

Software Setup

Jeff Rowberg has done excellent work in this area by creating a MPU-6050 Accelerometer / Gyro library. The Experiment makes use of this library. This library needs to be installed as given in the following steps:

Step 1: Download I2C dev library

Jeff Rowberg's I2C dev library is available at the following link:

https://github.com/jrowberg/i2cdevlib/tree/master/Arduino/I2Cdev

Step 2: Install I2C dev library

Copy I2C dev in the 'libraries' folder given by the path

C:\Program Files (x86)\Arduino\libraries

After copying, following files should be present in the folder C:\Program Files (x86)\Arduino\libraries\I2Cdev:

- I2Cdev.cpp
- I2Cdev.h

- keywords.txt
- library.json

Step 3: Download MPU-6050 library

Jeff Rowberg's MPU-6050 library is available at the following link:

https://github.com/jrowberg/i2cdevlib/tree/master/Arduino/MPU6050

Step 4: Install MPU-6050 library

Copy the MPU-6050 in the 'libraries' folder present in the path where Arduino IDE is installed. In our case the path was

C:\Program Files (x86)\Arduino\libraries

After copying, following files should be present in the folder C:\Program Files (x86)\Arduino\libraries\MPU6050:

- helper_3dmath.h
- library.json
- MPU6050.cpp
- MPU6050.h
- MPU6050_6Axis_MotionApps20.h
- MPU6050_9Axis_MotionApps41.h
- examples\ IMU_Zero\
    - \ MPU6050_DMP6\
    - \ MPU6050_DMP6_Ethernet\
    - \ MPU6050_raw\

This Experiment uses example sketches MPU6050_raw and MPU6050_DMP6 as reference.

Step 5: Set the baud-rate

Change the baud-rate of the Display monitor to 38400.

Sketch

```
// Accelerometer/Gyro based rotation control for DC motor
// This sketch considers MPU6050_raw example as reference
```

Experiment 8: Accelerometer based Rotation Control

```
/* ============================================================
I2Cdev device library code is placed under the MIT license
Copyright (c) 2011 Jeff Rowberg

Permission is hereby granted, free of charge, to any person obtaining a
copy of this software and associated documentation files (the
"Software"), to deal in the Software without restriction, including
without limitation the rights to use, copy, modify, merge, publish,
distribute, sublicense, and/or sell copies of the Software, and to permit
persons to whom the Software is furnished to do so, subject to the
following conditions:

The above copyright notice and this permission notice shall be included
in all copies or substantial portions of the Software.

THE SOFTWARE IS PROVIDED "AS IS", WITHOUT WARRANTY OF ANY
KIND, EXPRESS OR IMPLIED, INCLUDING BUT NOT LIMITED TO THE
WARRANTIES OF MERCHANTABILITY, FITNESS FOR A PARTICULAR
PURPOSE AND NONINFRINGEMENT. IN NO EVENT SHALL THE AUTHORS
OR COPYRIGHT HOLDERS BE LIABLE FOR ANY CLAIM, DAMAGES OR
OTHER LIABILITY, WHETHER IN AN ACTION OF CONTRACT, TORT OR
OTHERWISE, ARISING FROM, OUT OF OR IN CONNECTION WITH THE
SOFTWARE OR THE USE OR OTHER DEALINGS IN THE SOFTWARE.
============================================================
*/

#include "I2Cdev.h"
#include "MPU6050.h"

// Arduino Wire library is required if
// I2Cdev I2CDEV_ARDUINO_WIRE implementation is used in I2Cdev.h
#if I2CDEV_IMPLEMENTATION == I2CDEV_ARDUINO_WIRE
    #include "Wire.h"
#endif

// class default I2C address is 0x68
// specific I2C addresses may be passed as a parameter here
MPU6050 accelgyro ;
int16_t ax, ay, az ;
int16_t gx, gy, gz ;
const int pin1 = 3 ;
```

```
const int pin2 = 5 ;

void setup( )
{
    // initialize serial communication
    // 38400 chosen since it works as well at 8 MHz as it does at 16 MHz
    Serial.begin ( 38400 ) ;
    // Serial.begin ( 9600 ) ;

    // join I2C bus ( I2Cdev library doesn't do this automatically )
    #if I2CDEV_IMPLEMENTATION == I2CDEV_ARDUINO_WIRE
        Wire.begin( ) ;
        Serial.println ( "wire" ) ;
    #elif I2CDEV_IMPLEMENTATION == I2CDEV_BUILTIN_FASTWIRE
        Fastwire::setup ( 400, true ) ;
        Serial.println ( "fast wire" ) ;
    #endif

    // initialize device
    Serial.println ( "Initializing I2C devices..." ) ;
    accelgyro.initialize( ) ;

    // verify connection
    Serial.println ( "Testing device connections..." ) ;
    Serial.println ( accelgyro.testConnection( )
        ? "MPU6050 connection OK!" : "MPU6050 connection failed" ) ;

    pinMode ( pin1, OUTPUT ) ;
    pinMode ( pin2, OUTPUT ) ;
    delay ( 2000 ) ;
}

void loop( )
{
    // read raw accel/gyro measurements from device
    accelgyro.getMotion6 ( &ax, &ay, &az, &gx, &gy, &gz ) ;

    // other methods
    // accelgyro.getAcceleration ( &ax, &ay, &az ) ;
    // accelgyro.getRotation ( &gx, &gy, &gz ) ;
```

Experiment 8: Accelerometer based Rotation Control

```
ax = map ( ax, -20000, 20000, -2000, 2000 ) ;
ay = map ( ay, -20000, 20000, -2000, 2000 ) ;
az = map ( az, -20000, 20000, -2000, 2000 ) ;

// Individual ax, ay and az can be used depending on the application
// Used here is the sum of ax, ay, az components
int acclr = ax + ay + az ; // compute sum

// Serial.print ( ax ) ; Serial.print ( " " ) ;
// Serial.print ( ay ) ; Serial.print ( " " ) ;
// Serial.println ( az ) ;
// Serial.print ( gx ) ; Serial.print ( " " ) ;
// Serial.print ( gy ) ; Serial.print ( " " ) ;
// Serial.println ( gz ) ;

if ( acclr >= 0 && acclr <= 500 )
{
    Serial.println ( acclr ) ;
    // rotate
    analogWrite ( pin2 ,200 ) ;
    digitalWrite ( pin1, LOW ) ;
}
else if ( acclr > 500 )
{
    Serial.println ( "greater than +500" ) ;
    // MAX speed, rotate
    analogWrite ( pin2, 255 ) ;
    digitalWrite ( pin1, LOW ) ;
}
else if ( acclr >= -500 && acclr < 0 )
{
    Serial.println ( acclr ) ;
    // rotate in reverse direction
    analogWrite ( pin1, 200 ) ;
    digitalWrite ( pin2, LOW ) ;
}
else
{
    Serial.println ( "less than -500" ) ;
    // MAX speed, rotate in reverse direction
    analogWrite ( pin1 , 255 ) ;
```

```
        digitalWrite ( pin2 , LOW ) ;
   }

   delay ( 1000 ) ;
}
```

Result

- When the Sketch is executed, DC motor rotates at normal speed. The speed increases as MPU-6050 board is moved in a particular direction.
- When the MPU-6050 board is moved in a different direction, the motor reverses and speed increases if the change is substantial.
- The Display monitor prints the various messages including the range used for rotation of the motor.

Explanation

The global variable **accelgyro** is object of MPU6050. The other variables are **ax, ay, az, gx, gy, gz** are of the type **int16_t**. The type **int16_t** ensures that the integer is of 16 bits on any Arduino platform. The PWM pins used for DC motor control are 3 and 5 (represented by variables **pin1** and **pin2**).

The **setup( )** function does following:

- It initializes serial communication at 38400 baud rate using **Serial.begin( )**.
- Joins I2C bus when **Wire.begin( )** is invoked to have wire communication with MPU6050.
- Initializes I2C device, MPU6050 by calling **accelgyro.initialize( )**.
- Tests the connection by calling **accelgyro.testConnection( )**.
- The pins **pin1** and **pin2** are configured as OUTPUT using **pinMode( )**.

In the **loop( )** function **getMotion6( )** is invoked to get Accelerometer / Gyro values as given below:

accelgyro.getMotion6 (&ax, &ay, &az, &gx, &gy, &gz) ;

Experiment 8: Accelerometer based Rotation Control

These values are mapped in a range from (+20000 to -20000) to (-2000 to +2000) using **map( )** function.

The sketch uses **ax, ay** and **az** values for calculation of acceleration in x-direction, y-direction and z-direction respectively. The sketch just calculates the sum of all three values and stores it in **acclr** variable.

acclr is divided into different ranges and accordingly the motor rotates in forward direction or reverse direction. This is achieved through the code given below.

```
if ( acclr >= 0 && acclr <= 500 )
{
    Serial.println ( acclr ) ;
    // rotate
    analogWrite ( pin2 , 200 ) ;
    digitalWrite ( pin1 , LOW ) ;
}
else if ( acclr > 500 )
{
    Serial.println ( "greater than +500" ) ;
    // MAX speed, rotate
    analogWrite ( pin2 , 255 ) ;
    digitalWrite ( pin1 , LOW ) ;
}
else if ( acclr >= -500 && acclr < 0 )
{
    Serial.println ( acclr ) ;
    // rotate in reverse direction
    analogWrite ( pin1 , 200 ) ;
    digitalWrite ( pin2 , LOW ) ;
}
else
{
    Serial.println ( "less than -500" ) ;
    // MAX speed, rotate in reverse direction
    analogWrite ( pin1 , 255 ) ;
    digitalWrite ( pin2 , LOW ) ;
}
```

Functions Used

Some of the functions used in the sketch are already explained in previous chapters. The functions which are not yet explained are given below.

Arduino's wire implementation "Wire.h" is used in the sketch. The different functions that are part of Wire library are given below.

Wire.begin ( )
Initiate the Wire library and Join the I2C bus as a master
Wire.requestFrom (address, quantity, stop)
Used by the master to request bytes from a slave device.
address: the 7-bit address of the slave device.
quantity: the number of bytes to request.
stop : True or False (boolean).
Wire.beginTransmission (address)
Begins a transmission to the slave with the given address.
address: the 7-bit address of the slave device.
Wire.endTransmission (stop)
Ends transmission to a slave device and transmits the bytes that were queued.
stop : True or False (Boolean) .
Return: status of Transmission.
Wire.write (value)
Writes data from a slave device in response to a request from a master or queues bytes for transmission from a master to slave device in-between calls to **beginTransmission( )** and **endTransmission( )**.
value: a value to send as a single byte.
Return: the number of bytes written.

Experiment 8: Accelerometer based Rotation Control

> Wire.read( )
>
> Reads a byte that was transmitted from a slave device to a master after a call to **requestFrom( )** or was transmitted from a master to a slave.
>
> Return: The next byte received.

More Tweaks

- Develop a sketch to control DC motor and stabilize its vibrations based on example code given in MPU6050_DMP6 sketch of Jeff Rowberg's library.

- Following sketch gives an implementation using Euler angle support to control motor rotation direction based on MPU6050_DMP6 example. The following sketch makes use of **stabilized** flag. This flag is set to 1 after an interval of 10000 ms (i.e. 10 sec). This is done so that MPU6050 stabilizes in DMP mode for initial 10 seconds. One of the Euler angle (angle1) is used for motor control.

```
// MPU6050 DMP (Digital Motion Processor) based motor control
#include "I2Cdev.h"

#include "MPU6050_6Axis_MotionApps20.h"
// not necessary if using MotionApps include file
// #include "MPU6050.h"

// Arduino Wire library is required
// if I2Cdev I2CDEV_ARDUINO_WIRE implementation
// is used in I2Cdev.h
#if I2CDEV_IMPLEMENTATION == I2CDEV_ARDUINO_WIRE
    #include "Wire.h"
#endif

// class default I2C address is 0x68
// specific I2C addresses may be passed as a parameter here
// (default for SparkFun breakout and InvenSense evaluation board)
// AD0 low = 0x68
// AD0 high = 0x69
```

```
MPU6050 mpu ;
//MPU6050 mpu ( 0x69 ) ; // <-- use for AD0 high

// MPU control/status vars
// set true if DMP init was successful
bool dmpReady = false ;
// holds actual interrupt status byte from MPU
uint8_t mpuIntStatus ;
// return status after each device operation (0 = success, !0 = error)
uint8_t devStatus ;
// expected DMP packet size (default is 42 bytes)
uint16_t packetSize ;
// count of all bytes currently in FIFO
uint16_t fifoCount ;
// FIFO storage buffer
uint8_t fifoBuffer[ 64 ] ;

// orientation/motion vars
 // [w, x, y, z] quaternion container
Quaternion q ;
// [x, y, z] accel sensor measurements
VectorInt16 aa ;
// [x, y, z] gravity-free accel sensor measurements
VectorInt16 aaReal ;
// [x, y, z] world-frame accel sensor measurements
VectorInt16 aaWorld ;
// [x, y, z] gravity vector
VectorFloat gravity ;
// [psi, theta, phi] Euler angle container
float euler[ 3 ] ;
// [yaw, pitch, roll] yaw/pitch/roll container and gravity vector
float ypr[ 3 ] ;

// indicates whether MPU interrupt pin has gone high
volatile bool mpuInterrupt = false ;
void dmpDataReady( )
{
    mpuInterrupt = true ;
}

float angle1, angle2, angle3 ;
```

Experiment 8: Accelerometer based Rotation Control **91**

```
int pwmPin1 = 5 ;
int pwmPin2 = 3 ;
byte stabilized = 0 ;
#define OUTPUT_READABLE_EULER

void setup( )
{
    // join I2C bus ( I2Cdev library doesn't do this automatically )
    #if I2CDEV_IMPLEMENTATION == I2CDEV_ARDUINO_WIRE
        Wire.begin( ) ;
        TWBR = 24 ; // 400kHz I2C clock ( 200kHz if CPU is 8MHz )
    #elif I2CDEV_IMPLEMENTATION == I2CDEV_BUILTIN_FASTWIRE
        Fastwire::setup ( 400, true ) ;
    #endif

    // initialize serial communication

    // Serial.begin ( 115200 ) ;
    Serial.begin ( 38400 ) ;
    while ( !Serial )
        ;

    // initialize device
    Serial.println ( F ( "Initializing I2C devices..." ) ) ;
    mpu.initialize( ) ;

    // verify connection
    Serial.println ( F ( "Testing device connections..." ) ) ;
    Serial.println ( mpu.testConnection ( ) ?
        F ( "MPU6050 connection successful" )
        : F ( "MPU6050 connection failed" ) ) ;
    // wait for ready
    Serial.println ( F ( "\nSend any character to begin DMP programming
                    and demo: " ) ) ;
    // empty buffer
    while ( Serial.available( ) && Serial.read( ) )
        ;

    // wait for data
    while ( !Serial.available( ) )
        ;
```

```
// empty buffer again
while ( Serial.available( ) && Serial.read( ) )
    ;

// load and configure the DMP
Serial.println ( F ( "Initializing DMP..." ) ) ;
devStatus = mpu.dmpInitialize( ) ;

// supply your own gyro offsets here, scaled for min sensitivity
mpu.setXGyroOffset ( 220 ) ;
mpu.setYGyroOffset ( 76 ) ;
mpu.setZGyroOffset ( -85 ) ;
// 1688 factory default
mpu.setZAccelOffset ( 1788 ) ;

// make sure it worked ( returns 0 if so )
if ( devStatus == 0 )
{
    // turn on the DMP, now that it's ready
    Serial.println ( F ( "Enabling DMP..." ) ) ;
    mpu.setDMPEnabled ( true ) ;

    // enable Arduino interrupt detection
    Serial.println ( F ( "Enabling interrupt detection
            ( Arduino external interrupt 0 ) ..." ) ) ;
    attachInterrupt ( 0, dmpDataReady, RISING ) ;
    mpuIntStatus = mpu.getIntStatus( ) ;

    // set our DMP Ready flag so the main
    // loop( ) function knows it's okay to use it
    Serial.println ( F ( "DMP ready! Waiting for first interrupt..." ) ) ;
    dmpReady = true ;

    // get expected DMP packet size for later comparison
    packetSize = mpu.dmpGetFIFOPacketSize( ) ;
}
else
{
    // ERROR!
    // 1 = initial memory load failed
```

Experiment 8: Accelerometer based Rotation Control **93**

```
        // 2 = DMP configuration updates failed
        // ( if it's going to break, usually the code will be 1 )
        Serial.print ( F ( "DMP Initialization failed ( code " ) ) ;
        Serial.print ( devStatus ) ;
        Serial.println ( F ( " ) " ) ) ;
    }

    // DC Motor
    pinMode ( pwmPin1, OUTPUT ) ;
    pinMode ( pwmPin2, OUTPUT ) ;

}

void loop( )
{
    long currTime ;

    // if programming failed, don't try to do anything
    if ( !dmpReady )
        return ;

    // wait for MPU interrupt or extra packet ( s ) available
    while ( !mpuInterrupt && fifoCount < packetSize )
    {
    }

    // reset interrupt flag and get INT_STATUS byte
    mpuInterrupt = false ;
    mpuIntStatus = mpu.getIntStatus( ) ;

    // get current FIFO count
    fifoCount = mpu.getFIFOCount( ) ;

    // check for overflow
    // (this should never happen unless our code is too inefficient)
    if ( ( mpuIntStatus & 0x10 ) || fifoCount == 1024 )
    {
        // reset so we can continue cleanly
        mpu.resetFIFO( ) ;
        // Serial.println ( F ( "FIFO overflow!" ) ) ;
```

```
            // otherwise, check for DMP data ready interrupt
            // (this should happen frequently)
    }
    else if ( mpuIntStatus & 0x02 )
    {
            // wait for correct available data length,
            // should be a VERY short wait
            while ( fifoCount < packetSize )
                fifoCount = mpu.getFIFOCount( ) ;

            // read a packet from FIFO
            mpu.getFIFOBytes ( fifoBuffer, packetSize ) ;

            // track FIFO count here in case there is > 1 packet available
            // (this lets us immediately read more without waiting for an
            // interrupt)
            fifoCount -= packetSize ;

            #ifdef OUTPUT_READABLE_EULER
                // display Euler angles in degrees
                mpu.dmpGetQuaternion ( &q, fifoBuffer ) ;
                mpu.dmpGetEuler ( euler, &q ) ;
                currTime = millis ( ) ;
                // execute once, only for stabilization of Accelerometer/Gyro
                if ( stabilized == 0 && ( currTime > 10000 ) )
                {
                    mpu.dmpGetQuaternion ( &q, fifoBuffer ) ;
                    mpu.dmpGetEuler ( euler, &q ) ;
                    // set the stabilized flag
                    stabilized = 1 ;
                    Serial.println ( "Stabilized" ) ;
                }
                // Periodically reading Accelerometer/Gyro readings
                if ( stabilized == 1 )
                {
                    mpu.dmpGetQuaternion ( &q, fifoBuffer ) ;
                    mpu.dmpGetEuler ( euler, &q ) ;

                    angle1 = euler[0] * 180/M_PI ;
                    angle2 = euler[1] * 180/M_PI ;
                    angle3 = euler[2] * 180/M_PI ;
```

Experiment 8: Accelerometer based Rotation Control **95**

```
                if ( angle1 > 0.00 && angle1 < 180.00 )
                {
                    Serial.print ( " above 0 deg: " ) ;
                    Serial.println ( angle1 ) ;
                    // MAX speed - direction
                    setDir1 ( 255 ) ;
                    delay ( 1000 ) ;
                }
                else
                {
                    Serial.print ( " less than 0 deg: " ) ;
                    Serial.println ( angle1 ) ;
                    // MAX speed- reverse direction
                    setDir2 ( 255 ) ;
                    delay ( 1000 ) ;
                }
            }
        #endif
    }
}

void setDir1 ( int value )
{
    analogWrite ( pwmPin1, value ) ;
    digitalWrite ( pwmPin2 , LOW ) ;
}

void setDir2 ( int value )
{
    analogWrite ( pwmPin2 , value ) ;
    digitalWrite ( pwmPin1 , LOW ) ;
}
```

EXPERIMENT NINE

WIRELESS CONNECTIVITY

The business of business is relationships; the business of life is human connection.

- *Robin S. Sharma*

Experiment

This Experiment is about configuring a new ESP-8266 based wireless module to provide wireless connectivity to Arduino. This Experiment forms an important step to add wireless (WiFi) functionality via UART serial connection to the Arduino. The WiFi module supports 802.11 b/g/n protocol and an integrated TCP / IP protocol stack.

Hardware Setup

This Experiment needs an ESP-8266 breakout board and an Arduino Uno board. The breakout board is needed so that it can work with +5V supply from Arduino. These boards are shown in Figure 9.1 and 9.2.

Figure 9.1 ESP-8266 Breakout Board

Figure 9.2 Arduino Uno

Experiment 9: Wireless Connectivity 99

AT commands are used to interact with ESP-8266. AT stands for ATtention. Every command starts with "AT". "AT" is the prefix that informs ESP8266 about the start of command line. There are two ways to send AT commands to ESP-8266 from Arduino—either via Serial Monitor of Arduino IDE or via our sketch (during execution).

The steps to configure a **new** ESP-8266 module are given below:

Step 1: Pin connections shown in Figure 9.3 should be made.

Arduino Pins	ESP-8266 Board Pins
+5V	+5V
GND	GND
Digital pin 2	TX
Digital pin 3	RX

Figure 9.3 Pin connections

Step 2: Baud rate setting

Connect Arduino and open Serial Display monitor. Set the baud-rate of the monitor to 9600 baud and ensure "NL & CR" is selected. This is shown in the Figure 9.4.

Figure 9.4 Baud rate setting of serial monitor

Step 3a: Upload the following sketch and verify it with the message given in **Step 3b** in the next section.

Sketch

```
/* ESP8266 setup */
#include <SoftwareSerial.h>

// connect pin 2 to TX of esp8266,
// connect pin 3 to RX of esp8266
SoftwareSerial mySerial ( 2, 3 ) ;

void setup( )
{
    // Open serial communications and wait for port to open:
    Serial.begin ( 9600 ) ;
    while ( !Serial )
    {
        ; // wait for serial port to connect.
    }

    Serial.println ( "Perform Configuration!" ) ;

    // set the data rate for the SoftwareSerial port
    mySerial.begin( 115200 ) ; // 74880,57600, 38400,
                                // 19200, 9600, 4800
    mySerial.println ( "Hello, world.." ) ;
}

// run over and over
void loop( )
{
    if (mySerial.available( ) )
    {
        Serial.write ( mySerial.read( ) ) ;
    }
    if ( Serial.available( ) )
    {
        mySerial.write ( Serial.read( ) ) ;
```

Experiment 9: Wireless Connectivity 101

```
    }
}
```

Step 3b: Verify Message

After sketch is uploaded and executed following message should appear:

Perform Configuration!
Hello, world..
ERROR

Note the following code in the sketch:

mySerial.begin (115200) ; // 74880, 57600, 38400, 19200, 9600, 4800

Here the baud-rate is set at 115200. This is done as the fresh ESP-8266 from factory is expected to be set at 115200 baud-rate. However, after sketch is uploaded and executed and if message shown is not matching to what is given in the **Step 3b,** then change the baud-rate and perform the step again. Sometimes, changing of baud-rate is needed as the ESP-8266 module may have been set at different baud-rate. Continue to change to various baud-rates (like 74880, 57600, 38400, 19200, 9600, 4800) till you get the message exactly matching to the **Step 3b**.

Step 3c: Check AT command

Type AT in the Serial monitor and press "Send" button.
OK → should be the response in the Serial monitor.

Step 4: Set Baud-rate of ESP-8266

Type AT+UART=9600,8,1,0,0 and press "Send" button.

This step sets the baud-rate of ESP-8266 to 9600 baud. The baud-rate of 9600 is required for various experiments (that use ESP-8266 module) given in this book.

Step 5: Configure ESP-8266

Type AT+CWMODE=3 and press "Send" button. Specifying 3 configures ESP8266 module as AP station and Client.

Step 6: Get List of Access Points (APs)

Type AT+CWLAP and press "Send" button.

The module will return list of all active Access Points nearby. Identify your Access Point. A sample list of Access Points is shown in Figure 9.5.

```
COM29 (Arduino/Genuino Uno)
AT+CWLAP
AT+CWLAP
+CWLAP: (4,"UTkorde",-68,"00:1b:57:fc:17:4b",6,56,0)
+CWLAP: (4,"301DWARKA",-91,"00:17:7c:6c:28:92",6,25,0)
+CWLAP: (3,"BSNL WIFI",-92,"00:17:7c:72:2c:17",6,28,0)
+CWLAP: (3,"Dani",-85,"00:22:93:8f:69:39",11,16,0)
+CWLAP: (3,"D-Link",-86,"3c:1e:04:2a:99:9f",11,11,0)

OK
```

Figure 9.5 List of Access Points

Step 7: Connect to a Access Point

Type AT+CWJAP="Name of your access point", "your password" and press "Send" button. Wait for some time until module responds with "Wifi Connected".

A sample connection to Access Point is shown in Figure 9.6.

```
COM29 (Arduino/Genuino Uno)
    AT+CWJAP="UTkorde","xxxxx"
AT+CWLAP
+CWLAP: (4,"UTkorde",-68,"00:1b:57:fc:17:4b",6,56,0)
+CWLAP: (4,"301DWARKA",-91,"00:17:7c:6c:28:92",6,25,0)
+CWLAP: (3,"BSNL WIFI",-92,"00:17:7c:72:2c:17",6,28,0)
+CWLAP: (3,"Dani",-85,"00:22:93:8f:69:39",11,16,0)
+CWLAP: (3,"D-Link",-86,"3c:1e:04:2a:99:9f",11,11,0)

OK
AT+CWJAP="UTkorde","             "
WIFI DISCONNECT
WIFI CONNECTED
WIFI GOT IP

OK
```

Figure 9.6 Connection to Access Point

Experiment 9: Wireless Connectivity

Step 8: Find IP of the ESP-8266 module

Type AT+CIFSR and press "Send" button. The IP address allocated to ESP-8266 module is displayed (refer Figure 9.7).

```
COM29 (Arduino/Genuino Uno)

+CWLAP:(3,"Dani",-85,"00:22:93:8f:69:39",11,16,0)
+CWLAP:(3,"D-Link",-86,"3c:1e:04:2a:99:9f",11,11,0)

OK
AT+CWJAP="UTkorde","          "
WIFI DISCONNECT
WIFI CONNECTED
WIFI GOT IP

OK
AT+CIFSR
+CIFSR:APIP,"192.168.4.1"
+CIFSR:APMAC,"a2:20:a6:0f:75:2e"
+CIFSR:STAIP,"192.168.1.5"
+CIFSR:STAMAC,"a0:20:a6:0f:75:2e"

OK

Autoscroll
```

Figure 9.7 IP address allocated to ESP-8266 module

Result

Step 9: Ping

Open Command prompt and Ping to the IP that is assigned to ESP-8266 module. Ping should be successful as shown in the Figure 9.8.

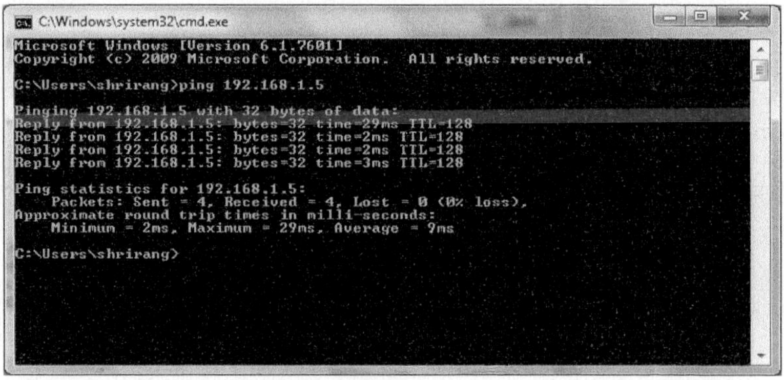

Figure 9.8 Ping to ESP-8266 module

Explanation

The sketch relies on the Software Serial library. Arduino hardware has built-in support for serial communication on pins 0 and 1 (TX & RX) which are used for serial communication with PC via the USB connection.

The Software Serial library allows serial communication to take place on other digital pins. It replicates the functionality of the hardwired RX and TX lines. Hence the sketch uses **"SoftwareSerial.h"** for communication between Arduino and ESP-8266.

Initially object (**mySerial**) of SoftwareSerial is created with pins as 2 and 3 as input to the constructor.

The **setup( )** function initializes serial communication with PC using **Serial.begin( )**. It also sets baud-rate for Software Serial port using **mySerial.begin( )**.

In the **loop( )** function, if data is available at the Software Serial port (means pins 2 and 3) then it is written to the Display monitor. Also, if the data is available from Serial display monitor (means pins 1 and 2 of Arduino), then it is written to the Software Serial port.

Experiment 9: Wireless Connectivity

Functions Used

Given below is a list of functions that have been used in this Experiment's sketch.

Serial.available( )
Gets the number of bytes (characters) available for reading from the serial port. Data that's already arrived and stored in the serial receive buffer (which holds 64 bytes).
Return: the number of bytes available to read.

Serial.write (val), Serial.write (str)
Writes binary data to the serial port.
Data is sent as a byte or series of bytes.
val: a value to send as a single byte.
str: a string to send as a series of bytes.
Return: the number of bytes written, (reading that number is optional).

Serial.read( )
Reads incoming serial data.
Return: the first byte of incoming serial data available (or -1 if no data is available).

SoftwareSerial : available( )
Gets the number of bytes (characters) available for reading from a software serial port. Data has already arrived and stored in serial receive buffer.
Return: the number of bytes available to read.

SoftwareSerial : begin (speed)
Sets the speed (baud-rate) for serial communication.
speed: the baud-rate as long.

SoftwareSerial : read( )

Returns a character that was received on the RX pin of the software serial port. Return: the character read or -1 if none is available.
SoftwareSerial : write (data) Prints data to the transmit pin of the software serial port as raw bytes. Working is same as the **Serial.write( )** function. Return: the number of bytes written, though reading that number is optional

More Tweaks

Study the following AT commands and configure ESP-8266 module as

- TCP client
- TCP server

AT commands to be used are AT+RST, AT+CIPSTART, AT+CIPSEND, AT+CIPCLOSE.

CHAPTER TEN

SEND EMAIL

Prior to email, our private correspondence was secured by a government institution called the postal service. Today, we trust AOL, Microsoft, Yahoo, Facebook, or Gmail with our private utterances.

- John Battelle

Experiment

This Experiment is about sending an email using Arduino and ESP-8266 module. The Experiment makes use of smtp2go service so that mails can be sent to an email address of your choice. smtp2go provides email services to send the emails using outgoing email server. This approach also allows us to send status of various sensors connected to Arduino (mentioned in various experiments) to a specific email address.

Hardware Setup

This Experiment needs an ESP-8266 breakout board and an Arduino Uno board. These are shown in Figure 10.1 and 10.2. The ESP-8266 module should be configured at 9600 baud as discussed in the previous experiment.

Figure 10.1 ESP-8266 Breakout Board

Experiment 10: Send email **109**

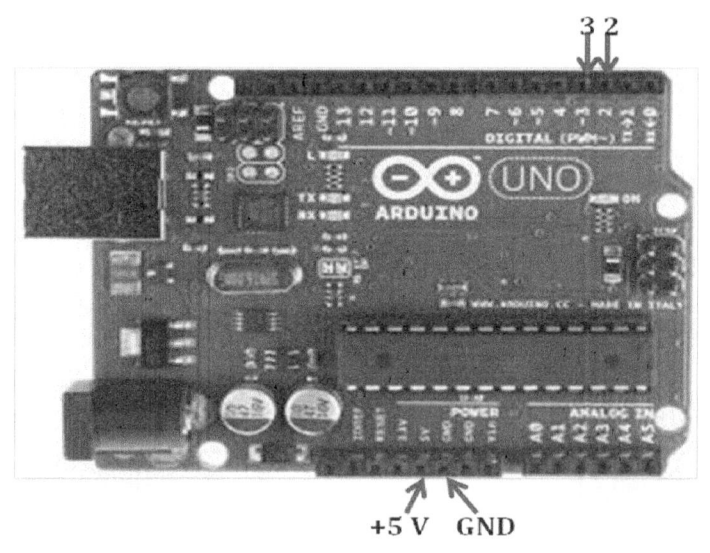

Figure 10.2 Arduino Uno

Pin connections shown in Figure 10.3 should be made.

Arduino Pins	ESP-8266 Board Pins
+5V	+5V
GND	GND
Digital pin 2	TX
Digital pin 3	RX

Figure 10.3 Pin connections

In addition to the usual Hardware Setup, we need to carry out the following steps to perform this Experiment:

- Sign Up at smtp2go.com.
- Create username and password in base64 encoded format with utf-8 character set.
- Write the sketch and upload it.
- Check for email in your account with subject as "Test mail".

These steps are discussed below in detail.

SMTP2GO Sign Up

smtp2go.com provides email services, to send the emails using outgoing email server. To avail these services you need to sign up for email address and password at https://www.smtp2go.com. This is shown in the Figure 10.4.

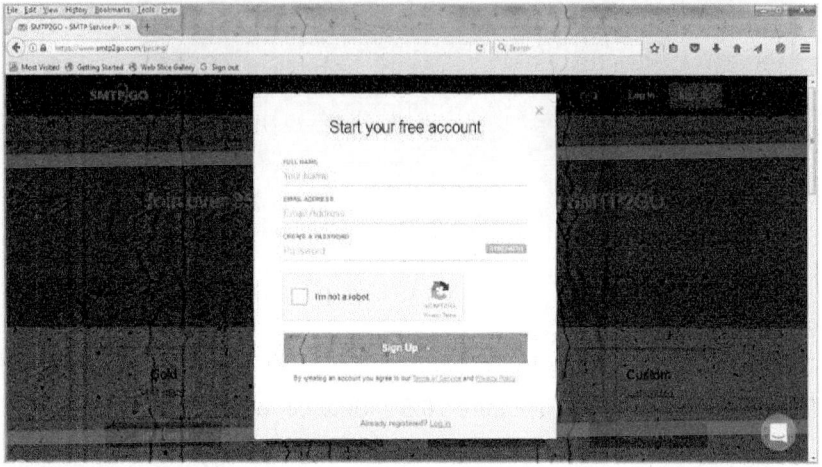

Figure 10.4 smtp2go.com signup

Encode Username and Password

To login at smtp2go.com through the sketch, username (email address can be used as username) and password are needed in base64 encoded format with utf-8 character set. This encoding can be done through https://www.base64encode.org/ as shown in Figure 10.5.

Experiment 10: Send email **111**

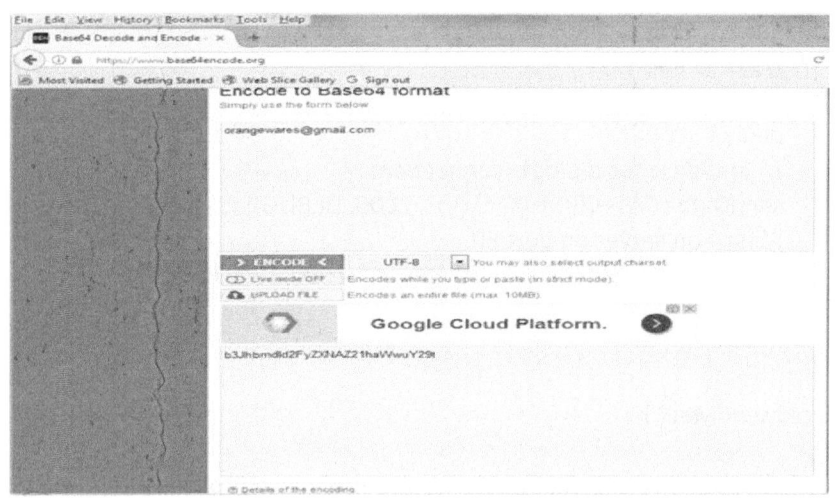

Figure 10.5 Encoding

Sketch

```
// Send Email from Arduino
#include <SoftwareSerial.h>
#define DEBUG true

// connect the TX line from ESP-8266 to Arduino's pin 2
// and the RX line from the ESP-8266 to Arduino's pin 3
SoftwareSerial esp8266 ( 2, 3 ) ;

void setup( )
{
    Serial.begin ( 9600 ) ;
    esp8266.begin ( 9600 ) ;
    Serial.println ( "Ready!!") ;

    // reset module
    sendData ( "AT+RST\r\n", 2000, DEBUG ) ;
    // configure as access point as well as station
    sendData ( "AT+CWMODE=3\r\n", 1000, DEBUG ) ;
    // Connect to your access point please type your own SSID and
    // password
    sendData ( "AT+CWJAP=\"UTkorde\", \"0123456789\"\r\n", 5000,
             DEBUG ) ;
```

```
    delay ( 3000 ) ;
    // get ip address
    sendData ( "AT+CIFSR\r\n", 3000, DEBUG ) ;
    delay ( 3000 ) ;
    // configure for multiple connections
    sendData ( "AT+CIPMUX=1\r\n", 2000, DEBUG ) ;
    // turn on server on port 80
    sendData ( "AT+CIPSERVER=1,80\r\n", 1000, DEBUG ) ;
    sendMail( ) ;
}

void sendMail( )
{
    sendDataln ( "AT+CIPSTART=4,\"TCP\",\"mail.smtp2go.com\",2525",
                 2000, DEBUG ) ;
    sendDataln ( "AT+CIPSEND=4,18", 2000, DEBUG ) ;
    // EHLO command
    sendDataln ( "EHLO 192.168.1.5", 2000, DEBUG ) ;
    sendDataln ( "AT+CIPSEND=4,12", 2000, DEBUG ) ;
    // AUTH command
    sendDataln ( "AUTH LOGIN", 2000, DEBUG) ;
    sendDataln ( "AT+CIPSEND=4,30", 2000, DEBUG ) ;
    // base64 encoded username
    // https://www.base64encode.org/
    sendDataln ( "b3Jhbmdld2FyZXNAZ21haWwuY29t", 2000, DEBUG ) ;
    // base64 encoded password
    // https://www.base64encode.org/
    sendDataln ( "AT+CIPSEND=4,14", 2000, DEBUG ) ;
    sendDataln ( "c210cDJnbw==", 2000, DEBUG ) ;
    sendDataln ( "AT+CIPSEND=4,35",2000, DEBUG ) ;
    // MAIL command, from email address
    sendDataln ( "MAIL FROM:<orangewares@gmail.com>", 2000,
                 DEBUG ) ;
    sendDataln ( "AT+CIPSEND=4,33", 2000, DEBUG ) ;
    // RCPT command , To email address
    sendDataln ( "RCPT To:<orangewares@gmail.com>", 2000, DEBUG );
    sendDataln ( "AT+CIPSEND=4,6", 2000, DEBUG ) ;
    // DATA command
    sendDataln ( "DATA", 2000, DEBUG ) ;
    sendDataln ( "AT+CIPSEND=4,20", 2000, DEBUG ) ;
    // Subject
```

Experiment 10: Send email **113**

```
        sendDataln ( "Subject: Test mail", 2000, DEBUG ) ;
        sendDataln ( "AT+CIPSEND=4,25", 2000, DEBUG ) ;
        // email body - content
        sendDataln ( "Test email from Arduino", 2000, DEBUG ) ;
        sendDataln ( "AT+CIPSEND=4,3", 2000, DEBUG ) ;
        sendDataln ( ".", 10000,DEBUG ) ;
        sendDataln ( "AT+CIPSEND=4,6", 2000, DEBUG ) ;
        // QUIT command
        sendDataln ( "QUIT", 2000, DEBUG ) ;
}

void loop( )
{
}


// Send data to ESP8266
// Params: command - the data/command to send
// timeout - the time to wait for a response
// debug - print to Serial window? (true = yes, false = no)
// Returns: The response from ESP8266 (if there is a response)
String sendData ( String command, const int timeout, boolean debug )
{
    String response = "" ;

    // send the read character to the esp8266
    esp8266.print ( command ) ;

    long int time = millis( ) ;

    while ( ( time + timeout ) > millis( ) )
    {
        while ( esp8266.available( ) )
        {
            // The esp has data so display its output to the serial window
            // read the next character
            char c = esp8266.read( ) ;
            response += c ;
        }
    }

    if ( debug )
```

```
    {
        Serial.print ( response ) ;
    }

    return response ;
}

// Send data to ESP8266 using println( )
// Params: command - the data/command to send
// timeout - the time to wait for a response
// debug - print to Serial window? (true = yes, false = no)
// Returns: The response from the ESP8266 (if there is a response)
String sendDataln ( String command, const int timeout, boolean debug )
{
    String response = "" ;

    // send the read character to the esp8266
    esp8266.println ( command ) ;

    long int time = millis( ) ;

    while ( ( time + timeout ) > millis( ) )
    {
        while ( esp8266.available( ) )
        {
            // The esp has data so display its output to the serial window
            // read the next character.
            char c = esp8266.read( ) ;
            response += c ;
        }
    }

    if ( debug )
    {
        Serial.print ( response ) ;
    }

    return response ;
}
```

Experiment 10: Send email **115**

Result

A mail should be delivered to the email address mentioned in the sketch. The subject line should be "Test mail" with contents in the email body. Figure 10.6 shows the email delivered from Arduino.

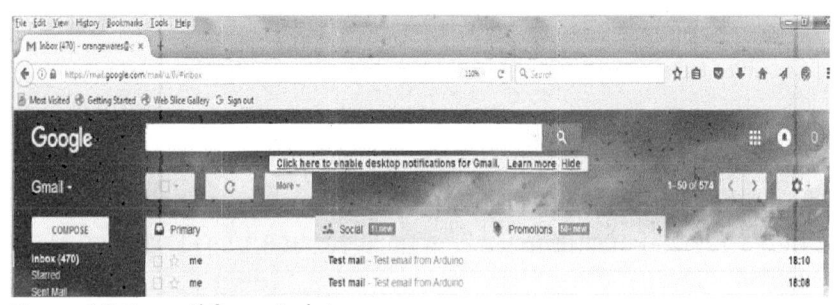

Figure 10.6 email from Arduino

The serial monitor output is shown in Figure 10.7.

```
Ready!!
AT+RST
OK
WIFI DISCONNECT
bBÖ†@üRcjþÂÉ¥SNÂÉ¥QNÂI?ë? ¤?BDç...ç?ü"?›€Í?²V‡¡?Cf²Ë‹C?
Ai-Thinker Technology Co. Ltd.

ready
AT+CWMODE=3
OK
AT+CWJAP="UTkorde"," XXXXXXXXXX"
WIFI DISCONNECT
WIFI CONNECTED
WIFI GOT IP
OK
AT+CIFSR
+CIFSR:APIP,"192.168.4.1"
+CIFSR:APMAC,"a2:20:a6:0f:75:2e"
+CIFSR:STAIP,"192.168.1.5"
+CIFSR:STAMAC,"a0:20:a6:0f:75:2e"
OK
```

```
AT+CIPMUX=1
OK
AT+CIPSERVER=1,80
OK
AT+CIPSTART=4,"TCP","mail.smtp2go.com",2525
4,CONNECT
OK
+IPD,4,70:220 mail.smtp2go.com ESMTP Exim 4.87 Sat, 05 Aug 2017
12:40:13 +0000
AT+CIPSEND=4,18
OK
>
Recv 18 bytes
SEND OK
+IPD,4,178:250-mail.smtp2go.com Hello 192.168.1.5 [117.198.90.1]
250-SIZE 52428800
250-8BITMIME
250-DSN
250-PIPELINING
250-AUTH CRAM-MD5 PLAIN LOGIN
250-STARTTLS
250-PRDR
250 HELP
AT+CIPSEND=4,12
OK
>
Recv 12 bytes
SEND OK
+IPD,4,18:334 VXNlcm5hbWU6
AT+CIPSEND=4,30
OK
>
Recv 30 bytes
SEND OK
+IPD,4,18:334 UGFzc3dvcmQ6
AT+CIPSEND=4,14
OK
>
Recv 14 bytes
SEND OK
+IPD,4,30:235 Authentication succeeded
```

Experiment 10: Send email **117**

```
AT+CIPSEND=4,35
OK
>
Recv 35 bytes
SEND OK
+IPD,4,8:250 OK
AT+CIPSEND=4,33
OK
>
Recv 33 bytes
SEND OK
+IPD,4,38:250 Accepted <orangewares@gmail.com>
AT+CIPSEND=4,6
OK
>
Recv 6 bytes
SEND OK
+IPD,4,56:354 Enter message, ending with "." on a line by itself
AT+CIPSEND=4,20
OK
>
Recv 20 bytes
SEND OK
AT+CIPSEND=4,25
OK
>
Recv 25 bytes
SEND OK
AT+CIPSEND=4,3
OK
>
```

Figure 10.7 Serial monitor output

Explanation

When you send an email, it doesn't go directly from your device to the recipient. Instead, it travels between many different computers on its way. Its first port of call is an SMTP server. In order to communicate with this server, you must use the SMTP protocol. SMTP (Simple Mail

Transfer Protocol) is the standard technology for sending email. This is simple and uses text-based protocol. Our sketch uses SMTP commands. A brief description of these commands is given below:

EHLO: This command is used to start the conversation. Underlying that the server is using the Extended SMTP protocol. It starts the conversation identifying the sender server and is generally followed by its domain name.

AUTH: With the AUTH command, the client authenticates itself to the server, giving its username and password. It's another layer of security to guarantee a proper transmission.

MAIL FROM: With this SMTP command, the sender states the source email address in the "From" field and actually starts the email transfer.

RCPT TO: It identifies the recipient of the email; if there are more than one, the command is simply repeated address by address.

DATA: With the DATA command the email content begins to be transferred. The subject can also be mentioned as part of data.

QUIT: It terminates the SMTP conversation.

The sketch relies on the Software Serial library. The Software Serial library allows serial communication to take place on digital pins other than 0 and 1. The sketch uses "SoftwareSerial.h" for communication between Arduino and ESP-8266.

Initially object **esp8266** of SoftwareSerial is created with pins as 2 and 3 as input to the constructor.

The **setup( )** function initializes serial communication with PC using **Serial.begin( )**. It also sets baud-rate for Software Serial port using **esp8266.begin( )**. Following steps are performed using calls to **sendData( )** function, to configure ESP-8266 module before it can be used for sending an email:

- Reset the ESP-8266 module using AT+RST command.
- Configure the ESP-8266 module to act as Access Point as well as station using AT+CWMODE=3 command.

Experiment 10: Send email **119**

- Connect the ESP-8266 module to your Access Point using the command AT+CWJAP=<SSID>,<password>.
- Get the IP address of ESP-8266 module using AT+CIFSR command.
- Configure ESP-8266 module for multiple connections using AT+CIPMUX=1 command.
- Configure ESP-8266 as TCP server and make it listen at port 80 using the command AT+CIPSERVER=1,80.

The **sendMail( )** function is used for sending the email. It makes use of **sendDataln( )** function. The **sendMail( )** function wraps the various SMTP commands. It also sends the username and password in base64 encoded form. The **sendMail( )** function is similar to **sendData( )** function, except it makes use of Software Serial **println( )** function. The working of **sendMail( )** function is given below.

It starts with the interaction with mail.smtp2go.com using TCP protocol on port 2525. In case this port is busy, other recommended ports which can be used are 8025, 587, 80, 465, 8465 and 443. This is shown below.

sendDataln ("AT+CIPSTART=4,\"TCP\",\"mail.smtp2go.com\",2525", 2000, DEBUG) ;

Here, 4 is the channel number used in the interaction.

The **EHLO** command is sent using the calls

sendDataln ("AT+CIPSEND=4,18", 2000, DEBUG) ;
sendDataln ("EHLO 192.168.1.5", 2000, DEBUG) ;

Here, 18 indicates character length of IP address + 2. 2 is added for \r and \n characters. The IP address specifies the domain name.

The **AUTH** command is sent using the calls

sendDataln ("AT+CIPSEND=4,12", 2000, DEBUG) ;
sendDataln ("AUTH LOGIN", 2000, DEBUG) ;

Here, 12 indicates the character length of "AUTH LOGIN" string + 2.

The base64 encoded username for smtp2go.com are sent as shown below.

sendDataln ("AT+CIPSEND=4,30", 2000, DEBUG) ;

sendDataln ("b3JhbmdId2FyZXNAZ21haWwuY29t", 2000, DEBUG) ;

Here, 30 indicates the character length of base64 encoded username + 2. Use your own user name in base64 encoded format and modify the character length accordingly.

The remaining code does the following:

The password in sent in the base64 encoded form. Use your password in base64 encoded format and modify the character length accordingly.

The **MAIL FROM** command is sent. Modify this suitably for your email address and its length.

The **RCPT TO** command is sent. Modify this suitably for your email address and its length.

The **DATA** command is sent.

The subject is sent.

The actual contents of the email are sent.

And finally after a long delay of 10,000 seconds, a **QUIT** command is sent.

To ensure that the sketch is executing correctly, compare its output with the output of serial monitor given in Figure 10.7.

The **sendData( )** and **sendDataln( )** functions are responsible for sending a command to ESP-8266 module. They make use of Software Serial **print( )** or **println( )** function. When current time obtained using **millis( )** exceeds the timeout value and if data is available on Software Serial port, then it reads the data and forms the response. DEBUG is set to "true" so that the ESP-8266 response can be printed on the serial monitor. The following code achieves this:

```
esp8266.print ( command ) ;
long int time = millis( ) ;
while ( ( time + timeout ) > millis( ) )
{
    while ( esp8266.available( ) )
    {
        char c = esp8266.read( ) ;
        response += c ;
    }
}
```

Experiment 10: Send email

Functions Used

Given below is a list of functions that have been used in this Experiment's sketch.

> SoftwareSerial : print (data), SoftwareSerial:println (data)
>
> Print data to the transmit pin of the software serial port. These functions are similar to **Serial.print( )** and **Serial.println( )**.
>
> Return: number of bytes written. Reading that number is optional.

More Tweaks

Modify the sketch to send the email to multiple email addresses.

EXPERIMENT ELEVEN

DIGITAL CLOCK

What interests me about clocks is that everything is hand-made, and yet to the person looking at the clock, something magical is happening that cannot be explained unless you are the clockmaker.

- *Brian Selznick*

Experiment

This Experiment is about creating a simple digital clock using LCD display. The idea is inspired the way in which a battery operated clock (or analog clock) requires setting of time when we start using it. Various time settings can be made using the push-button switches.

Hardware Setup

This Experiment needs Application board, LCD display panel and Arduino Uno board. These are shown in the Figures 11.1, 11.2 and 11.3.

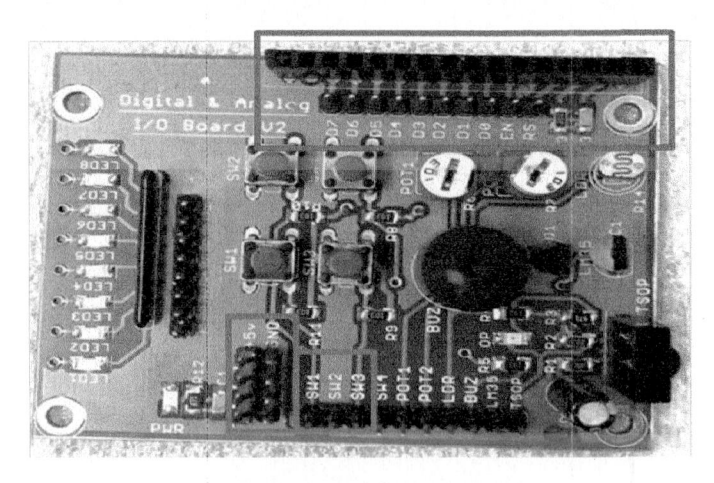

Figure 11.1 Application Board

Experiment 11: Clock **125**

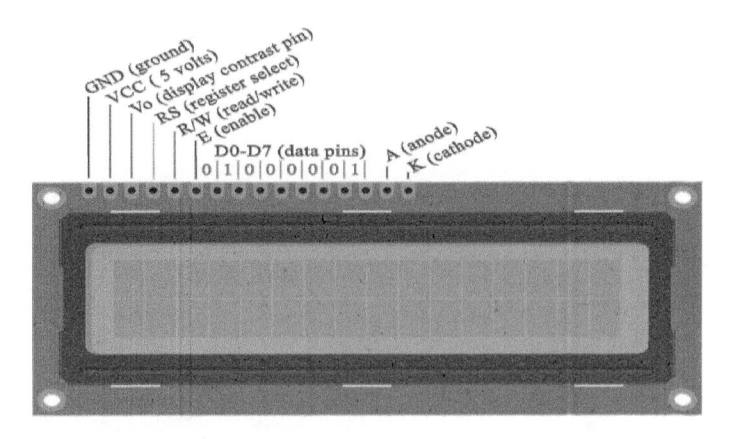

Figure 11.2 LCD panel

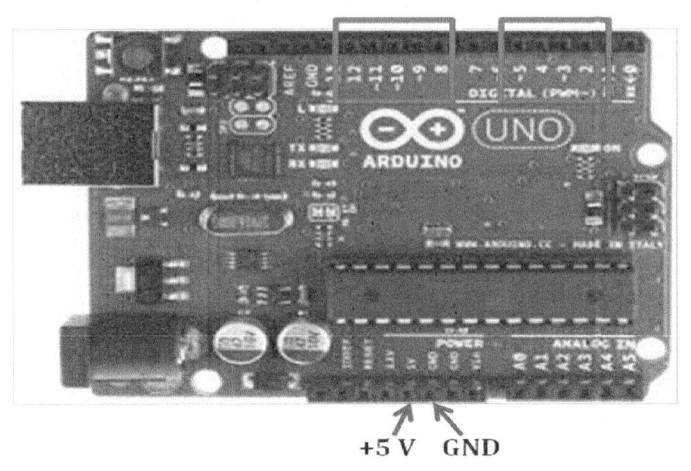

Figure 11.3 Arduino Uno

LCD panel should be connected with the Application board as shown in the Figure 11.4. The LCD panel with pins is inserted in the socket strip of Application board.

Figure 11.4 LCD panel connections with Application board

The external power adapter should be used to supply power to Arduino board. Alternately, you can insert batteries in the battery holder and connect it to supply external power. Supplying external power is necessary. Without it, the text on LCD panel may appear dim.

Pin connections shown in Figure 11.5 should be made.

Experiment 11: Clock **127**

Arduino Pins	Application Board Pins
+5V	+5V
GND	GND
Digital pin 8	SW 1
Digital pin 9	SW 2
Digital pin 10	SW 3
Digital pin 11	EN (E)
Digital pin 12	RS
Digital pin 5	D4
Digital pin 4	D5
Digital pin 3	D6
Digital pin 2	D7

Figure 11.5 Pin connections

Sketch

```
// Basic Digital Clock

#include <LiquidCrystal.h>
LiquidCrystal lcd ( 12, 11, 5, 4, 3, 2 ) ;
int hr = 0 ;
int mins = 0 ;
int sec = 0 ;
const int hourPin = 8 ;
const int minPin = 9 ;
const int ampmPin = 10 ;
// Flag to set AM or PM
bool ampmFlag = true ;
int switch1 ;
int switch2 ;
int switch3 ;

void setup( )
{
    Serial.begin ( 9600 ) ;
```

```
    lcd.begin ( 16, 2 ) ;
}

void loop( )
{
    lcd.setCursor ( 0, 0 ) ;
    // increment seconds
    sec = sec + 1 ;
    lcd.print ( "TIME:" ) ;
    lcd.print ( hr ) ;
    lcd.print ( ":" ) ;
    lcd.print ( mins ) ;
    lcd.print ( ":" ) ;
    lcd.print ( sec ) ;

    // show AM or PM based on flag value
    if ( ampmFlag )
        lcd.print ( "AM" ) ;
    else
        lcd.print ( "PM" ) ;

    delay ( 1000 ) ;
    lcd.clear( ) ;

    // increment mins
    if ( sec == 60 )
    {
        sec = 0 ;
        mins = mins + 1 ;
    }
    // increment hour
    if ( mins == 60 )
    {
        mins = 0 ;
        hr = hr + 1 ;
    }
    if ( hr == 13 )
        hr = 0 ;  // set to 0

    lcd.setCursor ( 0, 1 ) ;
    lcd.print ( "SET: SW1,SW2,SW3" ) ;
```

Experiment 11: Clock **129**

```
// Set Time using SW1, SW2, SW3
switch1 = digitalRead ( hourPin ) ;

if ( switch1 == 0 )
{
    hr = hr + 1 ;
    if ( hr >= 13 )
        hr = 0 ;
}
switch2 = digitalRead ( minPin ) ;
if ( switch2 == 0 )
{
    sec = 0 ;
    mins = mins + 1 ;
}

switch3 = digitalRead ( ampmPin ) ;
if ( switch3 == 0 )
{
    ampmFlag = !ampmFlag ;
}
}
```

Result

The digital clock is shown on LCD panel with Time as 0:0:0 AM.

- Press Switch 1 and hour will change. Hold the switch till the desired hour value is shown on the LCD panel.
- Press Switch 2 and minutes will change. Hold the switch till the desired minute value is shown on the LCD panel.
- Press Switch 3, to toggle between AM and PM.

Explanation

To use the LCD display, LiquidCrystal library is required. The "LIquidCrystal.h" file provides function required to use LCD panel with Arduino.

The LiquidCrystal object **lcd**'s constructor requires pins for using LCD (Digital pin 12 – RS pin and Digital pin 11 – EN pin) and the associated data pins (5, 4, 3, 2).

The variables **hr, mins** and **sec** are used for hour, minutes and seconds. The **hourPin** is used to set hour by reading Switch 1, **minPin** is used to set minutes by reading Switch 2 and **ampmPin** is used to set AM / PM by reading Switch 3. The **ampmFlag** variable is used to control setting of AM / PM. The variables **switch1, switch2** and **switch3** are used for storing Switch values.

In the **setup( )** function, serial LCD interface is initialized by calling the **lcd.begin( )** function.

In the **loop( )** function, the LCD cursor is set using **lcd.setCursor( )**. It is initialized to top left (0, 0) position. Next, the value of **seconds** is incremented. The string "TIME" followed by value of hours, minutes and seconds is printed. ":" is used as a separator. AM or PM is printed depending on the value of **ampmFlag**. The **lcd.print( )** function is used for printing the values.

A delay of 1 second (1000 ms) follows. After this the contents of LCD are cleared by calling the **lcd.clear( )** function. Minutes are incremented if seconds reach 60 and seconds are set to 0. This is achieved using the following code:

```
if ( sec == 60 )
{
   sec = 0 ;
   mins = mins + 1 ;
}
```

Similarly, hour is incremented when minutes reach 60 and **mins** is set to 0. This is achieved using the following code:

```
if ( mins == 60 )
{
   mins = 0 ;
   hr = hr + 1 ;
}
```

If **hr** value crosses 13, it is reset to 0.

Experiment 11: Clock

The cursor of LCD panel is set at row - 1 using **lcd.setCursor( )**. A message is displayed at **row - 1** indicating that use of SW1, SW2 and SW3 be used to set the clock to appropriate time.

Switch 1, Switch 2 and Switch3 are read using **digitalRead( )** function. When Switch 1 is pressed **hr** is incremented and if it becomes 13 then its value is reset to 0. Similarly, setting of minutes and seconds is handled. The AM / PM setting is handled by toggling **ampmFlag**. This is shown in the following code:

```
switch1 = digitalRead ( hourPin ) ;
if ( switch1 == 0 )
{
    hr = hr + 1 ;
    if ( hr >= 13 )
        hr = 0 ;
}
switch2 = digitalRead ( minPin ) ;
if ( switch2 == 0 )
{
    sec = 0 ;
    mins = mins + 1 ;
}
switch3 = digitalRead ( ampmPin ) ;
if ( switch3 == 0 )
{
    ampmFlag = !ampmFlag ;
}
```

Functions Used

The important functions used in this Experiment's sketch are given below.

LiquidCrystal : begin (cols, rows)

Initializes the interface to the LCD screen. Specifies the dimensions (width and height) of the display.

begin( ) needs to be called before any other LCD library commands.

cols: the number of columns that the display has.

---

rows: the number of rows that the display has.
LiquidCrystal : print (data)   Prints text to the LCD.   data: the data to print (char, byte, int, long, or string).
LiquidCrystal : clear( )   Clears the LCD screen and positions the cursor in the top-left corner.
LiquidCrystal : setCursor(col, row)   Positions the LCD cursor. Used to set the location at which subsequent text written to the LCD will be displayed.   col: column at which to position the cursor (0 is first column).   row: row at which to position the cursor (0 is first row).

More Tweaks

1. Develop a sketch to glow LED1 to LED8 one by one and display the corresponding string "LED1 glowing", "LED2 glowing", etc. on the LCD panel.

2. Reverse the glowing from LED8 to LED1 one by one and display the corresponding message on the LCD panel.

3. Use scrolling feature of LCD to scroll an appropriate string for each glowing LED.

EXPERIMENT TWELVE

WAMP SERVER BASED TEMPERATURE LOGGER

Today, Web services are really about developing for the server. What it means to developers is any set of systems services that you make a Web service you to access by any kind of device with a highly interactive client, not just a browser.

- John Fowler

Experiment

This Experiment is about logging temperature data on the custom WAMP server. The WAMP server can be hosted within intranet (or internet) on a Windows machine. The temperature data is collected using temperature sensor connected to Arduino board. Using the wireless connectivity to WAMP server, the data can be logged on the server in a file.

Hardware Setup

This Experiment needs an ESP-8266 board, Application Board and Arduino Uno board. These are shown in Figures 12.1, 12.2 and 12.3.

Figure 12.1 ESP-8266 board

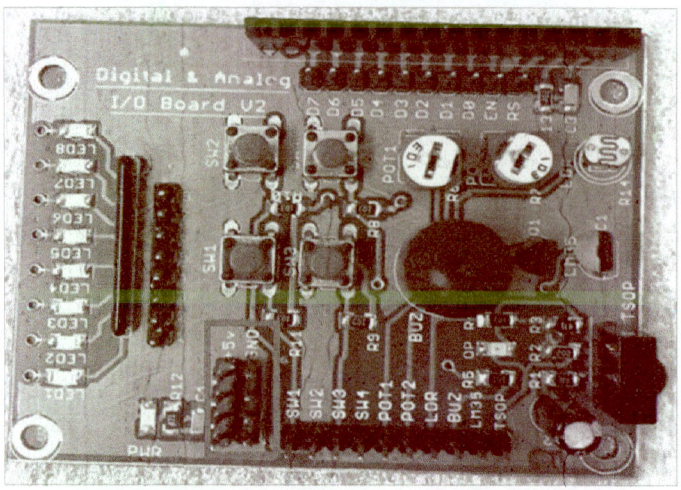

Figure 12.2 Application Board

Experiment 12 :WAMP based Temperature Logger 135

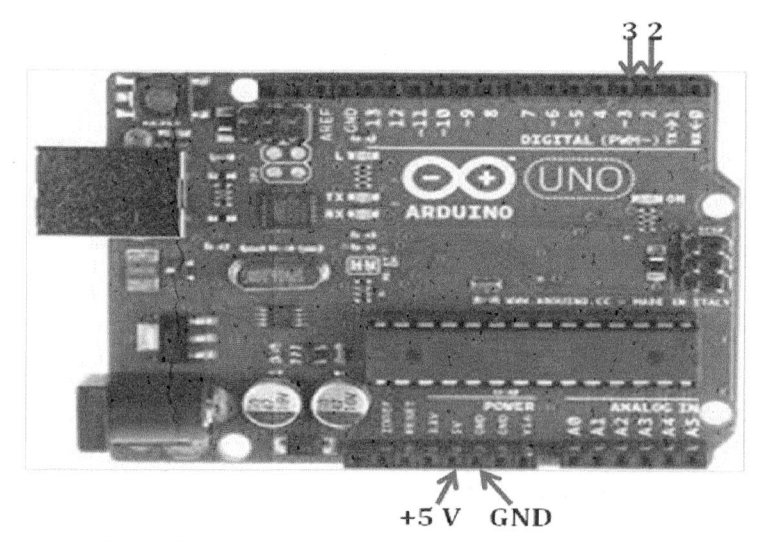

Figure 12.3 Arduino Uno

Pin connections shown in Figure 12.4 should be made.

Arduino Pins	ESP-8266 Board Pins
Digital pin 2	TX
Digital pin 3	RX

Arduino Pins	Application Board Pins
+5V	+5 V
GND	GND
A0	LM35

Application Board Pins	ESP-8266 Board Pins
+5V	+5V
GND	GND

Figure 12.4 Pin connections

Software Setup

The WAMP (Windows Apache MySQL Php) server is a Windows web development environment. It allows creation of web applications with Apache2, PHP and a MySQL database on a Windows machine.

Following steps should be carried out for WAMP installation:

1. Go to link http://www.wampserver.com/en/ and download WAMP Server 3.0.x installer. Choose either 64-bit Windows or 32-bit Windows, depending on OS on your machine.

2. Double click on WAMP Server installer and install the server via setup wizard.

    (a) Accept the license agreement.

    (b) Choose the installation directory.

    (c) Choose Create desktop icon.

    (d) Click on install button.

    (e) During installation, default browser (e.g FireFox) would be shown as detected. It is recommended to select it.

    (f) Do not change the Mail parameters. Click Next.

    (g) Press Finish button to complete the installation and to launch the WAMP Server.

Experiment 12 : WAMP based Temperature Logger

(h) Go the notification area, click on WAMP server icon and open the menu (server menu) and click on localhost option. This should open WAMP server home page in the default browser (i.e FireFox) as shown in the Figure 12.5. You should see the tools phpInfo and phpmyadmin.

Figure 12.5 WAMP Server Home Page

Create folder named 'Projects" under the www folder of the WAMP installation. For example, D:\wamp64\www\Projects.

3. Type the code given in the PHP Code section below, in a text editor, and save the file as ArduinoServer.php.

4. Copy the ArduinoServer.php file in the Projects folder.

5. Start All services of the WAMP server (via notification area).

PHP Code

```
<html>
<head>
<title>Receiver</title>
<?php
if ( isset ( $_GET[ 'temp1' ] ) )
{
```

```php
        $var1 = $_GET[ 'temp1' ] ;
        print ( "The temperature is ".$var1 ) ;
        $fileContent = "Temperature is ".$var1."\n" ;
        $fileStatus = file_put_contents ( 'myFile.txt', $fileContent,
                    FILE_APPEND ) ;
        if ( $fileStatus != false )
        {
            echo "Success" ;
        }
        else
        {
            echo "Fail" ;
        }
    }
    else
    {
        echo "Data not set" ;
    }
    ?>
    </head>
        <body>
        </body>
    </html>
```

Sketch

```cpp
// Temp Logger on WAMP server
// Set the appropriate IP address of WAMP server
// variable strIPaddr is used for IP address

#include <SoftwareSerial.h>
#include <stdlib.h>

#define DEBUG true
// LED
int ledPin = 13 ;
// LM35 analog input: A0 pin
int lm35Pin = 0 ;

// connect 2 to TX of Serial USB
```

Experiment 12 : WAMP based Temperature Logger

```
// connect 3 to RX of serial USB
SoftwareSerial esp8266 ( 2, 3 ) ;

// IP address of WAMP server hosting Apache, php page
// set IP address correctly
String strIPaddr = "192.168.1.2" ;

// this runs once
void setup( )
{
    // initialize the digital pin as an output
    pinMode ( ledPin, OUTPUT ) ;
    // enable debug serial
    Serial.begin ( 9600 ) ;
    // enable software serial
    esp8266.begin ( 9600 ) ;
    // reset module
    sendData ( "AT+RST\r\n", 2000, DEBUG ) ;
    // configure as access point as well as station
    sendData ( "AT+CWMODE=3\r\n", 1000, DEBUG ) ;
    // Connect to your access point, please type your own SSID
    // and password
    sendData ( "AT+CWJAP=\"UTkorde\",\"0123456789\"\r\n",
                5000, DEBUG ) ;
    delay ( 3000 ) ;
    // get ip address
    sendData ( "AT+CIFSR\r\n", 3000, DEBUG ) ;
    delay ( 1000 ) ;
}

// the loop
void loop( )
{
    // blink LED on board
    digitalWrite ( ledPin, HIGH ) ;
    delay ( 200 ) ;
    digitalWrite ( ledPin, LOW ) ;

    // read the value from LM35
    // read 10 values for averaging
    int val = 0 ;
```

```
for ( int i = 0; i < 10; i++ )
{
    val += analogRead ( lm35Pin ) ;
    delay ( 500 ) ;
}

// convert to temp:
// temp value is in 0-1023 range
// LM35 outputs 10mV/degree C. ie, 1 Volt => 100 degrees C
// So Temp = ( avg_val / 1023 ) * 5 Volts * 100 degrees / Volt
float temp = val * 50.0f / 1023.0f ;

// convert to string
String strTemp = String ( temp, 1 ) ;
Serial.println ( strTemp ) ;

// TCP connection
String cmd = "AT+CIPSTART=\"TCP\",\"" ;
cmd += strIPaddr ; //IP of WAMP server
cmd += "\",80" ;
esp8266.println ( cmd ) ;

if ( esp8266.find ( "Error" ) )
{
    Serial.println ( "AT+CIPSTART error" ) ;
    return ;
}

// prepare GET string
String getStr = "GET /projects/ArduinoServer.php" ;
getStr += "?temp1=" ;
getStr += strTemp ;
getStr += " HTTP/1.1\r\nHost: " ;
getStr += strIPaddr ;
getStr += "\r\n\r\n" ;

// Serial.println ( getStr ) ;
// send data length
cmd = "AT+CIPSEND=" ;
cmd += String ( getStr.length( ) ) ;
esp8266.println ( cmd ) ;
```

```
        if ( esp8266.find ( ">" ) )
        {
            esp8266.print ( getStr ) ;
        }
        else
        {
            esp8266.println ( "AT+CIPCLOSE" ) ;
            // alert user
            Serial.println ( "AT+CIPCLOSE" ) ;
        }

        // needs 15 sec delay between updates
        delay ( 16000 ) ;
}

String sendData ( String command, const int timeout, boolean debug )
{
    String response = "" ;
    // send the read character to the esp8266
    esp8266.print ( command ) ;

    long int time = millis( ) ;
    while ( ( time + timeout ) > millis( ) )
    {
        while ( esp8266.available( ) )
        {
            // The esp has data so display its output to the serial window
            // read the next character.
            char c = esp8266.read( ) ;
            response += c ;
        }
    }

    if ( debug )
    {
        Serial.print ( response ) ;
    }

    return response ;
}
```

Result

When the Arduino sketch is run, the ESP-8266 initializations are done. Then the temperature is shown on the display monitor. The temperature is shown on continuous basis. The temperature values are also sent to WAMP server. On the WAMP server php script is executed and it logs the temperature in the "myFile.txt". The display monitor output is shown below:

```
AT+RST
OK
WIFI DISCONNECT
bBÖ†øRcœþÂÉ¥SNÂÉ¥SNÂІ◌◌ ¤◌BDç1à◌÷S◌›€Íò–$×Ã†Cš◌ÐÁ–Àþ
Ai-Thinker Technology Co. Ltd.
ready
AT+CWMODE=3
OK
WIFI CONNECTED
AT+CWJAP="UTkorde","XXXXXXXXXX"
WIFI DISCONNECT
WIFI CONNECTED
WIFI GOT IP
OK
AT+CIFSR
+CIFSR:APIP,"192.168.4.1"
+CIFSR:APMAC,"a2:20:a6:0f:75:2e"
+CIFSR:STAIP,"192.168.1.3"
+CIFSR:STAMAC,"a0:20:a6:0f:75:2e"

OK
37.6
37.5
37.6
38.9
38.3
38.5
39.1
```

Experiment 12 :WAMP based Temperature Logger **143**

The sample temperature values logged to "MyFile.txt" are shown below.

D:\wamp64\www\Projects\myFile.txt

```
Temperature is 37.6
Temperature is 37.5
Temperature is 37.6
Temperature is 38.9
Temperature is 38.3
Temperature is 38.5
Temperature is 39.1
```

Explanation

The **lm35Pin** is used to store temperature sensor values read from A0 pin. The sketch relies on the Software Serial library. This library allows serial communication to take place on digital pins other than 0 and 1. The sketch uses "SoftwareSerial.h" for communication between Arduino and ESP-8266. Initially, object **esp8266** of **SoftwareSerial** is created, with pins as 2 and 3 as input to the constructor.

The **setup( )** function initializes serial communication with PC using **Serial.begin( )**. It also sets baud-rate for Software Serial port using **esp8266.begin( )**. The method **sendData( )** is used for configuring ESP-8266. Following steps should be performed to configure ESP-8266 module before it can be used for sending mail.

- Reset the ESP-8266 module using AT+RST command.

- Configure the ESP-8266 module to act as Access point as well as station using AT+CWMODE=3 command.

- Connect the ESP-8266 module to your Access Point using your SSID and password. The command is AT+CWJAP=<SSID>,<password>.

- Get the IP of ESP-8266 module using AT+CIFSR command.

The variable **strIpaddr** is used for storing the IP address of WAMP server. Before the sketch can be used, IP address should be set correctly.

In the **loop( )** function, the temperature readings are taken in a loop (10 readings) and an average value is calculated from these 10 readings. The temperature range and change of voltage per degree change are also considered while calculating the average temperature. This value is then converted to a string and sent to the WAMP server. It is also printed on the display monitor. The statements that achieve this are shown below.

```
float temp = val * 50.0f / 1023.0f ;
String strTemp = String ( temp, 1 ) ;
Serial.println ( strTemp ) ;
```

The TCP connection is established with the WAMP server and port 80 using command "AT+CIPSTART" as shown below. If an error occurs, it is shown on the display monitor through statements given below.

```
String cmd = "AT+CIPSTART=\"TCP\",\"" ;
cmd += strIPaddr ;
cmd += "\",80" ;
esp8266.println ( cmd ) ;

if ( esp8266.find ( "Error" ) )
{
    Serial.println ( "AT+CIPSTART error" ) ;
    return ;
}
```

The GET string is prepared for sending temperature data to the WAMP server. HTTP 1.1 protocol is used for sending the GET request. This is shown below.

```
String getStr = "GET /projects/ArduinoServer.php" ;
getStr += "?temp1=" ;
getStr += strTemp ;
getStr += " HTTP/1.1\r\nHost: " ;
getStr += strIPaddr ;
getStr += "\r\n\r\n" ;
```

The "AT+CIPSEND" command and the length of the data are now sent. In the response from WAMP server, ">" is searched. If it is found, the string **getStr** is sent to WAMP server. If ">" is not found, then it's an error and the connection with server is closed. This is shown below.

```
cmd = "AT+CIPSEND=" ;
```

Experiment 12 : WAMP based Temperature Logger

```
cmd += String( getStr.length() ) ;
esp8266.println( cmd ) ;
if ( esp8266.find ( ">" ) )
{
    esp8266.print ( getStr ) ;
}
else
{
    esp8266.println ( "AT+CIPCLOSE" ) ;
    Serial.println ( "AT+CIPCLOSE" ) ;
}
```

Functions Used

Given below is a list of functions that have been used in this project's sketch.

String (val), String (val, base), String (val, decimalPlaces)
Constructs an instance of the String class.
val: The value to format as a String. Value can be char, byte, int, long, unsigned int, unsigned long, float or double.
base (optional): The base in which to format the value.
decimalPlaces (only if val is float or double): Desired decimal places.
Returns: An instance of the String class.
string.length( )
Returns the length of the string.
string: a variable of type String.
SoftwareSerial : find (target)
Reads data from the serial buffer until the target string of given length is found.
target: The string to search for.
Return: The function returns true if target string is found, false if it times out.

More Tweaks

1. Develop a Arduino sketch and php script to control the LED (or DC motor) from WAMP server.
2. Develop a Arduino sketch and php script to update temperature values. If the temperature value exceeds a particular threshold then glow a LED on application board.
   - Hint: Use ESP-8266 first in TCP client mode (Single connection mode) and then as TCP server (Multiple connections mode) to receive commands from server (php script).
   - The php script should send control signal so that LED can be made to glow.

EXPERIMENT THIRTEEN

INTERNET / INTRANET BASED LED CONTROL

There was a time when people felt the internet was another world, but now people realize it's a tool that we use in this world.

- Tim Berners-Lee

Experiment

In the IoT scenario it is expected to control devices remotely over Internet / Intranet. This Experiment is about controlling LEDs over Internet / Intranet using a web interface. Since controlling using Internet requires a static IP address for the server, this Experiment demonstrates the same concept over Intranet.

Hardware Setup

This Experiment needs an ESP-8266 board, Application Board and Arduino Uno board. These are shown in Figures 13.1, 13.2 and 13.3.

Figure 13.1 ESP-8266 Board

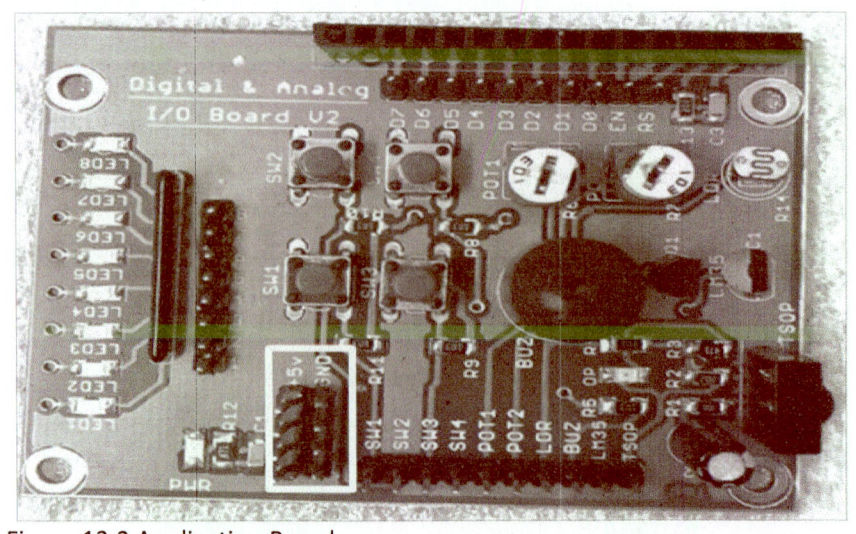

Figure 13.2 Application Board

Experiment 13: Intranet based LEDs Control **149**

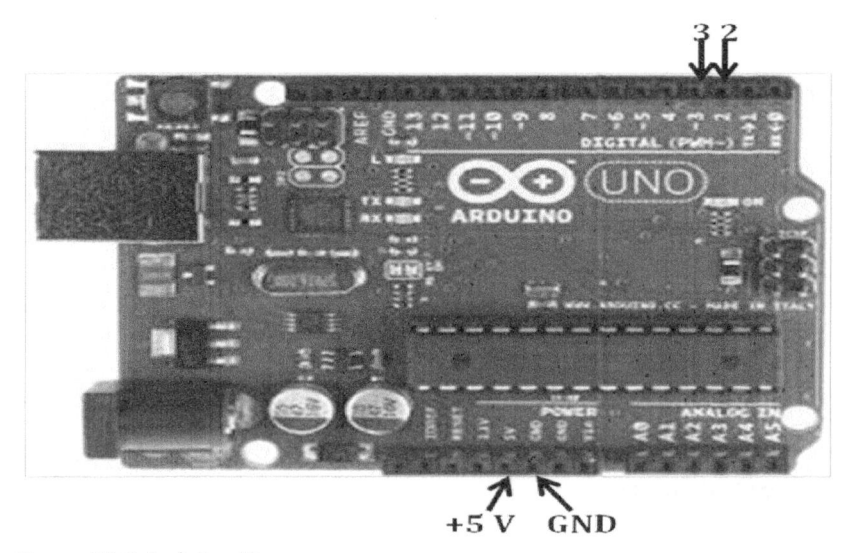

Figure 13.3 Arduino Uno

Pin connections shown in Figure 13.4 should be made.

Arduino Pins	ESP-8266 Board Pins
Digital pin 2	TX
Digital pin 3	RX

Application Board Pins	ESP-8266 Board Pins
+5 V	+5V
GND	GND

Arduino Pins	Application Board Pins
+5V	+5 V
GND	GND
Digital pin 11	LED1
Digital pin 12	LED2
Digital pin 13	LED3

Figure 13.4 Pin connections

Software Setup

Prepare a HTML page with three buttons. The page also includes a jquery library to handle button clicks. The library is needed for sending the http requests to ESP-8266 module. Following steps are required as part of web page setup:

(a) Open notepad (/notepad++) editor and type the code given in the HTML Code section below. Save the file to a folder, say, D:\LED_Control\LEDControl.html.

(b) Download jquery library from https://code.jquery.com/. A version jquery-1.1x.x.min.js serves the purpose. However higher versions can also be tried.

(c) Copy the jquery library to the same folder D:\LED_Control\jquery-1.1x.x.min.js

(d) Set the IP address of ESP-8266 module correctly in the html file. This is very important step. The HTTP request is sent to this IP address. So ensure that this is set correctly.

HTML Code

```
<html>
    <head>
        <title>Intranet based LED Control</title>
```

Experiment 13: Intranet based LEDs Control

```html
</head>
<body>

<!-- in the <button> tags below the ID attribute is the value
sent to the arduino -->

<!-- buttons for pin 11, pin 12, pin13 -->
<button id="11" class="led">Toggle Pin 11</button>
<button id="12" class="led">Toggle Pin 12</button>
<button id="13" class="led">Toggle Pin 13</button>

<script src="jquery-1.10.2.min.js"></script>
<script type="text/javascript">
$ ( document ).ready ( function( ) {
      //alert ( "inside ready" ) ;
   } ) ;
$ ( ".led" ).click ( function( ) {
var p = $ ( this ).attr ( 'id' ) ; // get id value (pin13, pin12, or pin11)
// alert ( p ) ;
// send HTTP GET request to the IP address with the parameter
// "pin" and value "p", then execute the function
$.get ( "http://192.168.43.139:80/", { pin:p } ) ; // execute get req.
      } ) ;
</script>
</body>
</html>
```

Sketch

```
// Intranet Controlled LEDs

#include <SoftwareSerial.h>
#define DEBUG true

// make RX Arduino line as pin 2, make TX Arduino line as pin 3
// connect the TX line from the esp to the Arduino's pin 2
// connect the RX line from the esp to the Arduino's pin 3
SoftwareSerial esp8266 ( 2,3 ) ;

void setup( )
```

```
{
    Serial.begin ( 9600 ) ;

    // set baudrate for comm with esp8266
    esp8266.begin ( 9600 ) ;

    // LED1
    pinMode ( 11,OUTPUT ) ;
    digitalWrite ( 11,LOW ) ;

    // LED2
    pinMode ( 12,OUTPUT ) ;
    digitalWrite ( 12,LOW ) ;

    // LED3
    pinMode ( 13,OUTPUT ) ;
    digitalWrite ( 13,HIGH ) ;

    sendData ( "AT+RST\r\n", 2000, DEBUG ) ; // reset module
    // configure as access point as well as station
    sendData ( "AT+CWMODE=3\r\n", 1000, DEBUG ) ;
    // Connects access point please type your own SSID and password
    sendData( "AT+CWJAP=\"UTkorde\", \"XXXXX\"\r\n", 5000, DEBUG);
    delay ( 3000 ) ;
    // get ip address
    sendData ( "AT+CIFSR\r\n", 3000, DEBUG ) ;
    delay ( 3000 ) ;
    // configure for multiple connections
    sendData ( "AT+CIPMUX=1\r\n", 2000, DEBUG ) ;
    // turn on server on port 80
    sendData ( "AT+CIPSERVER=1,80\r\n", 1000, DEBUG ) ;
}

void loop( )
{
    if ( esp8266.available( ) ) // check if the esp is sending a message
    {
        if ( esp8266.find ( "+IPD," ) )
        {
            // wait for the serial buffer to fill up ( read all serial data )
            delay ( 1000 ) ;
```

Experiment 13: Intranet based LEDs Control

```
            // get the connection id which is used for disconnection
            // subtract 48 because the read( ) function returns the ASCII
            // value and 0 (the first decimal number) starts at 48
            int connectionId = esp8266.read( ) - 48 ;

            // advance cursor to "pin="
            esp8266.find ( "pin=" ) ;

            // get first number
            // if pin 12 then the 1st number is 1, then multiply to get 10
            int pinNumber = ( esp8266.read( ) - 48 ) * 10 ;

            // get second number
            // if the pin number is 12 then the 2nd number is 2,
            // then add to the first number
            pinNumber += ( esp8266.read( ) - 48 ) ;

            // toggle pin
            digitalWrite ( pinNumber, !digitalRead ( pinNumber ) ) ;

            // make close command
            String closeCommand = "AT+CIPCLOSE=" ;
            // append connection id
            closeCommand += connectionId ;
            closeCommand += "\r\n" ;
            // close connection
            sendData ( closeCommand, 1000, DEBUG ) ;
        }
    }
}

// Sends data to ESP8266
// Parameters:
// command - the data/command to send
// timeout - the time to wait for a response
// debug - print to Serial window? (true = yes, false = no)
// Returns: The response from the esp8266 (if there is a response)
String sendData ( String command, const int timeout, boolean debug )
{
    String response = "" ;
```

```
// send the read character to the esp8266
esp8266.print ( command ) ;
long int time = millis( ) ;

while ( ( time + timeout ) > millis( ) )
{
    while ( esp8266.available( ) )
    {
        // The esp has data so display its output to the serial window
        // read the next character
        char c = esp8266.read( ) ;
        response += c ;
    }
}

if ( debug )
{
    Serial.print ( response ) ;
}

return response ;
}
```

Result

When the Arduino sketch is run, following things happen:

- Ready message is shown on the display monitor.
- AT commands are shown on the display monitor.
- IP address of ESP-8266 module is shown on the monitor.
- ESP 8266 is configured as TCP server to receive commands over net on port 80.
- LED1 and LED2 are glowing and LED3 is OFF.

Open the HTML page in the Browser. Ensure that IP address of ESP-8266 is correctly added to HTML script. Press the buttons to toggle LEDs. See the effect on LED toggling. Permit a delay of few seconds, before the effect takes place.

Experiment 13: Intranet based LEDs Control **155**

Explanation

About HTML Page

In the html page the head and body tags are defined. The title tag is used for giving the title of the Experiment. In the body tag 3 buttons are defined with a specific id and with an attribute class. The script is given below:

<button id="11" class="led">Toggle Pin 11</button>
<button id="12" class="led">Toggle Pin 12</button>
<button id="13" class="led">Toggle Pin 13</button>

The jquery library is included as shown in script below:

<script src="jquery-1.10.2.min.js"></script>

The **click( )** function gets invoked when a button is pressed. The class attribute "led" is used to have uniform response for various button clicks. This function uses the attribute "id" for deciding which button has been pressed and accordingly issues a HTTP GET request to the ESP-8266 module. This request is made by calling the **get( )** function. IP address and pin are sent as parameters to **get( )** function. The following part of the HTML script achieves this functionality:

$ (".led").click (function( ){
          var p = $ (this).attr ('id') ;
          $.get ("http://192.168.43.139:80/", {pin:p}) ;
     }) ;

About Arduino sketch

The sketch relies on the Software Serial library. This library allows serial communication to take place on digital pins other than 0 and 1. The sketch uses "SoftwareSerial.h" for communication between Arduino and ESP-8266. Initially, object **esp8266** of SoftwareSerial is created, with pins as 2 and 3 as input to the constructor.

The **setup( )** function initializes serial communication with PC using **Serial.begin( )**. It also sets baud-rate for Software Serial port using **esp8266.begin( )**. The digital pins 11, 12 and 13 are configured as

OUTPUT using **pinMode( )** function. The **digitalWrite( )** functions sets these pins either HIGH or LOW. The pin set to LOW will make LED1 and LED2 to glow and pin set to HIGH will make LED3 off as part of setup. The method **sendData( )** is used for configuring ESP-8266. Following steps are performed to configure ESP-8266 module before it can be used:

- Reset the ESP-8266 module using AT+RST command.

- Configure the ESP-8266 module to act as Access Point as well as station, using AT+CWMODE=3 command.

- Connect the ESP-8266 module to your Access Point using your SSID and password. The command is AT+CWJAP=<SSID>,<password>.

- Get the IP address of ESP-8266 module using AT+CIFSR command.

- Configure the ESP-8266 to have multiple connections. The command is AT+CIPMUX=1.

- Configure the ESP-8266 to act as server with port 80 being used for communication with client. The command is AT+CIPSERVER=1,80.

In the **loop( )** function a check is performed, whether ESP-8266 is sending any message. This can happen when a control command (via HTTP **get( )**) is received by ESP-8266 module. If the message is available, then search for "+IPD," pattern is done. If this succeeds then read is performed to get connection Id. A variable **connnectionId** is used to store the value after subtraction of 48 to get the decimal number. Then reading is advanced to find "pin=" pattern. The following code achieves this:

```
if ( esp8266.find ( "+IPD," ) )
{
    delay ( 1000 ) ;

    int connectionId = esp8266.read( ) - 48 ;
    esp8266.find ( "pin=" ) ;
    ...
}
```

Experiment 13: Intranet based LEDs Control **157**

The pin number is read in the variable **pinNumber**. This is done in two steps. Firstly, most significant digit is read and is multiplied by 10 to get ten's digit. This is followed by reading unit place's digit and sum is performed to obtain the actual pin number. After this, the pin is toggled using **digitalWrite( )** function which results in corresponding LED getting toggled. This is achieved through the code given below.

```
int pinNumber = ( esp8266.read( ) - 48 ) * 10 ;
pinNumber += ( esp8266.read( ) - 48 ) ;
digitalWrite ( pinNumber, !digitalRead ( pinNumber ) ) ;
```

Finally, the connection is closed by issuing the close command using **connectionId**.

Functions Used

Given below is a list of functions that have been used in this Experiment's sketch.

$ (document).ready( )
A ready event which fires up when HTML document is ready.
Code included inside **$ (document).ready( )** will run once Document is ready for javascript code to execute.
$ (selector).click( )
A click event occurs when an element is clicked. **click( )** method attaches a function to run when a click event occurs.
HTTP get( )
Sends an HTTP GET request to a server and gets back the result.
$.get (URL[, data][, function( )][, dataType])
URL: a string containing the URL to which request is sent.
data: Optional, specifies data to send to the server along with request.
function( ): Optional, specifies a function to run if request succeeds. Function can take parameters.
dataType: Optional, specifies the data type expected of the server response.

More Tweaks

Develop an Arduino sketch and HTML page with javascript code to control all the 8 LEDs.

EXPERIMENT FOURTEEN

PUBLIC IoT BASED TEMPERATURE LOGGER WITH TWEETS

Twitter isn't a social network, it's an information network.

- *Evan William*

Experiment

This Experiment collects the temperature data and logs it to a public IoT platform called ThingSpeak. ThingSpeak provides a structured way of accessing the data. It also links the logged data with social network platform Twitter. This allows receiving tweets for the user-defined conditions.

Hardware Setup

This Experiment needs an ESP-8266 board, Application Board and Arduino Uno board. These are shown in Figures 14.1, 14.2 and 14.3.

Figure 14.1 ESP-8266 Board

Figure 14.2 Application Board

Experiment 14 : Public IoT based Temperature Logger   161

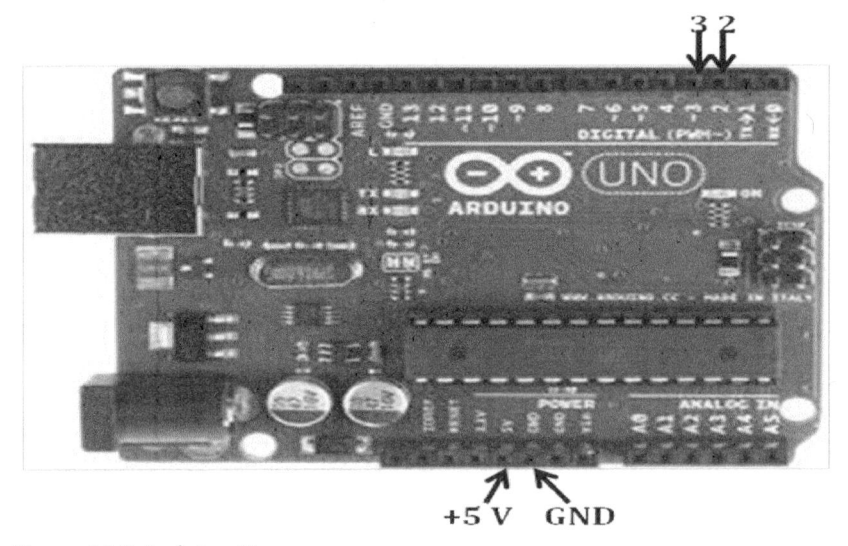

Figure 14.3 Arduino Uno

Pin connections shown in Figure 14.4 should be made.

Arduino Pins	ESP-8266 Board Pins
Digital pin 2	TX
Digital pin 3	RX

Arduino Pins	Application Board Pins
+5V	+5 V
GND	GND
A0	LM35

Application Board Pins	ESP-8266 Board Pins
+5V	+5V
GND	GND

Figure 14.4 Pin connections

Software Setup

To perform the experiment following steps have to be carried out:

Step 1: Create MathWorks account

- ThingSpeak is a public IOT platform maintained by a company called MathWorks. To use this platform we need to first create a Mathworks account by carrying out the steps given below.
- Go to www.thingspeak.com.
- Click on Sign Up from the menu at top.
- Create an account with an appropriate email address, username and password.
- As part of verification process, you will receive an email from MathWorks. Click on the button in this email to verify your valid email address.
- Once the email address is verified, your MathWorks account would be created.

Step 2: Create a new Channel

- Visit www.thingspeak.com and Sign In using the email and password of the MathWorks account that you have created.
- Click on Channels | New Channel. A channel is where one can monitor and log data.
- Enter channel details like "Name", "Description" and "Field1" as shown in Figure 14.5.

Experiment 14 : Public IoT based Temperature Logger 163

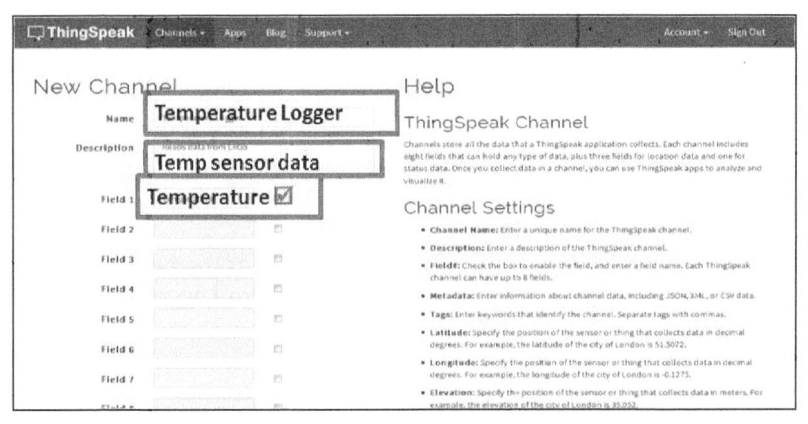

Figure 14.5 Channel details

- Save the channel by clicking on the Save Channel button present at the bottom of the page.
- Note the Channel Id and Write API key (from API Keys Tab). Those shown in Figure 14.6 are just for reference. In the Arduino sketch you would have to use the Write API key that was generated for you.

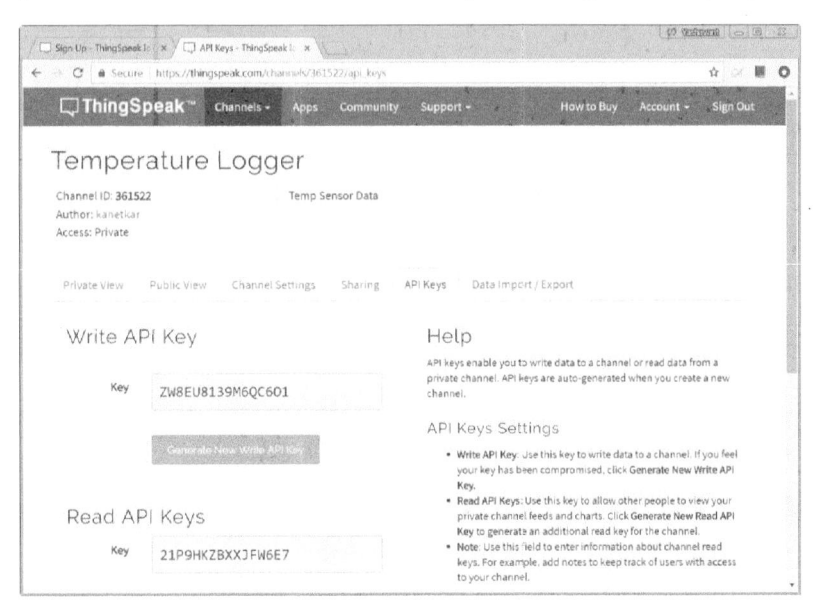

Figure 14.6 Temperature Logger along with Write API Key

Step 3: Execute Sketch

Make the connections and Upload the Arduino sketch shown in the next section. Don't forget to replace the Write API Key shown in the sketch with the one that was generated from your MathWorks account.

Step 4: Watch Temperature Logger

Watch temperature on ThingSpeak Temperature Logger's Private View. This is shown in Figure 14.7.

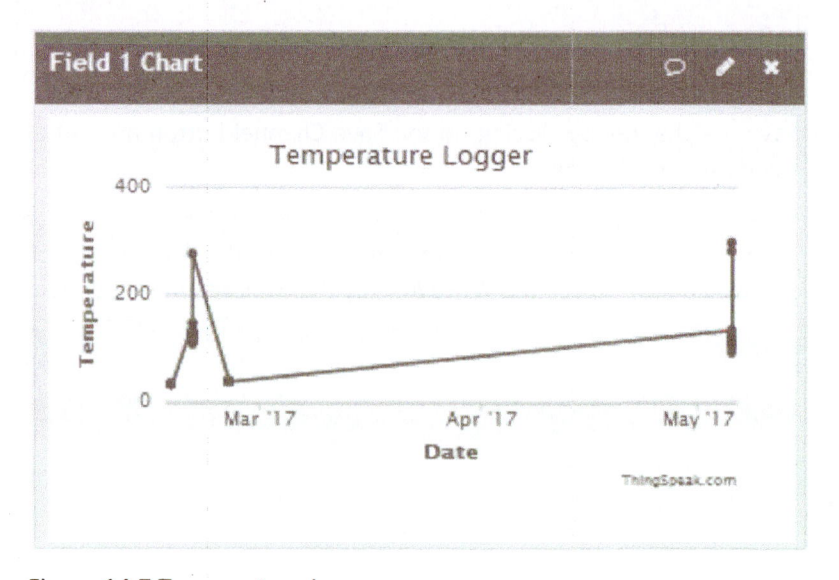

Figure 14.7 Temperature Logger

Step 5: Make channel public

By default the channel (i.e. Temperature Logger) is private. To let it be accessible to anybody carry out the following steps:

- Go to "Sharing" tab.
- Select "Share channel view with everyone".
- Select Public View tab to view the public temperature logger as shown in Figure 14.8.

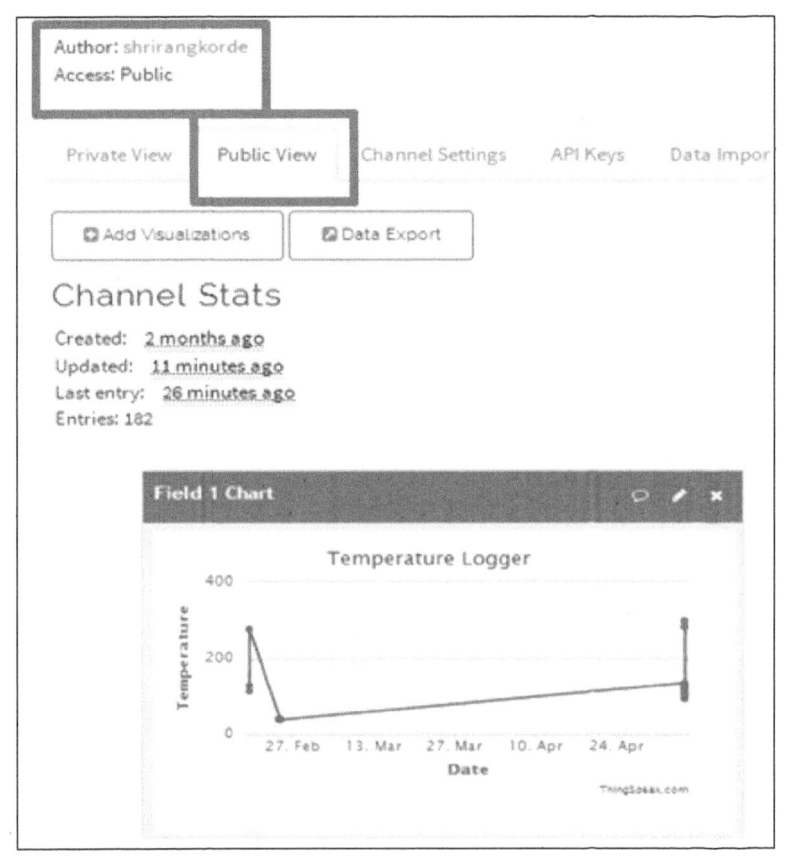

Experiment 14 : Public IoT based Temperature Logger **165**

Figure 14.8 Public Temperature Logger

Sketch

```
// Temperature Logger - ThingSpeak
#include <SoftwareSerial.h>
#include <stdlib.h>
#define DEBUG true

// LED
int ledPin = 13 ;
// LM35 analog input
int lm35Pin = A0 ;

// replace with your channel's API key
String apiKey = "9B7RATVU5176R79C" ;
```

```
// connect 2 to TX of Serial USB
// connect 3 to RX of serial USB
SoftwareSerial ser ( 2, 3 ) ; // RX, TX

void setup( )
{
    // initialize the digital pin as an output.
    pinMode ( ledPin, OUTPUT ) ;

    // enable debug serial
    Serial.begin ( 9600 ) ;
    // enable software serial
    ser.begin ( 9600 ) ;

    // reset ESP8266
    sendData ( "AT+RST\r\n", 2000, DEBUG ) ;
    // configure as access point as well as station
    sendData ( "AT+CWMODE=3\r\n", 1000, DEBUG ) ;
    // Connect to your access point, please type your own SSID and
    // password
    sendData ( "AT+CWJAP=\"UTkorde\", \"XXXXXXXXXX\"\r\n", 5000,
            DEBUG ) ;
    delay ( 3000 ) ;
    sendData ( "AT+CIFSR\r\n", 3000, DEBUG ) ;  // get ip address
    delay ( 1000 ) ;
    sendData ( "AT+CIPMUX=0\r\n", 2000, DEBUG ) ; // single conn.
}

void loop( )
{
    // blink LED on board
    digitalWrite ( ledPin, HIGH ) ;
    delay ( 200 ) ;
    digitalWrite ( ledPin, LOW ) ;

    // read the value from LM35.
    // read 10 values for averaging.
    int val = 0 ;
    for ( int i = 0 ; i < 10 ; i++ )
    {
```

Experiment 14 : Public IoT based Temperature Logger

```
        val += analogRead ( lm35Pin ) ;
        delay ( 500 ) ;
}

// convert to temp:
// temp value is in 0-1023 range
// LM35 outputs 10mV/degree C. ie, 1 Volt => 100 degrees C
// Temp = ( avg_val / 1023 ) * 5 Volts * 100 degrees / Volt
float temp = val * 50.0f / 1023.0f ;

// convert temperature to string
String strTemp = String ( temp, 1 ) ;
Serial.println ( strTemp ) ;

// TCP connection
String cmd = "AT+CIPSTART=\"TCP\",\"" ;
cmd += "184.106.153.149" ; // api.thingspeak.com
cmd += "\",80" ;
ser.println ( cmd ) ;

if ( ser.find ( "Error" ) )
{
    Serial.println ( "AT+CIPSTART error" ) ;
    return ;
}

// prepare GET string
String getStr = "GET /update?api_key=" ;
getStr += apiKey ;
getStr += "&field1=" ;
getStr += String ( strTemp ) ;
getStr += "\r\n\r\n" ;

// send data length
cmd = "AT+CIPSEND=" ;
cmd += String ( getStr.length( ) ) ;
ser.println ( cmd ) ;

if ( ser.find ( ">" ) )
{
    ser.print ( getStr ) ;
```

```
    }
    else
    {
        ser.println ( "AT+CIPCLOSE" ) ;
        // alert user
        Serial.println ( "AT+CIPCLOSE" ) ;
    }

    // thingspeak needs 15 sec delay between updates
    delay ( 16000 ) ;
}

String sendData ( String command, const int timeout, boolean debug )
{
    String response = "" ;
    // send the read character to the esp8266
    ser.print ( command ) ;
    long int time = millis( ) ;

    while ( ( time + timeout ) > millis( ) )
    {
        while ( ser.available( ) )
        {
            // read the next character
            char c = ser.read( ) ;
            response += c ;
        }
    }

    if ( debug )
    {
        Serial.print ( response ) ;
    }

    return response ;
}
```

Experiment 14 : Public IoT based Temperature Logger **169**

Twitter Alerts

We now have a publically viewable Temperature logger in place. Let us now connect it to our Twitter account to generate Twitter alerts. To achieve this carry out the following steps:

Step 1: Generate Twitter Alerts

- Go to Apps menu and scroll to ThingTweet in the Actions section of the page. Click on ThingTweet button.

- Click on Link Twitter Account button.

- Click on Authorize app button to authorize ThingTweet to use your Twitter account. Ensure that you have a twitter account.

- Note the API key for linking Twitter account as shown in Figure 14.9.

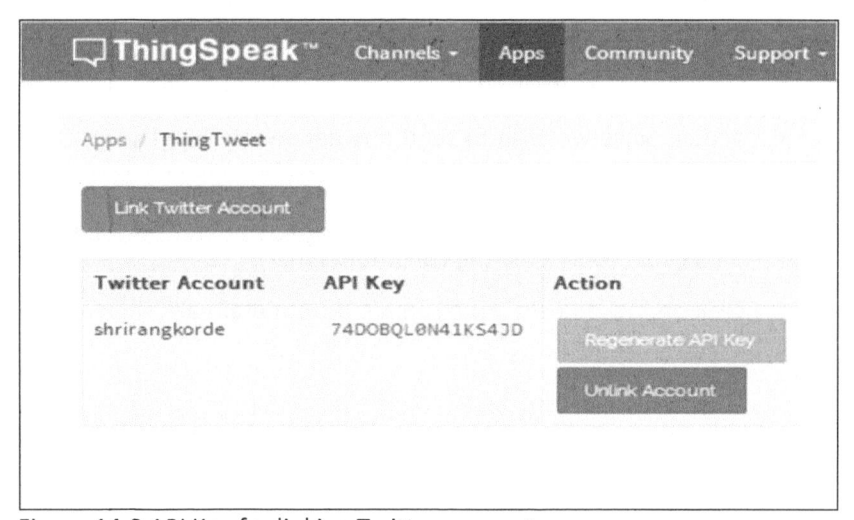

Figure 14.9 API Key for linking Twitter account

Step 2: Link to React

- Go to Apps menu and scroll down to React button in Actions section of the page. Click on React button followed by New React button as shown in Figure 14.10.

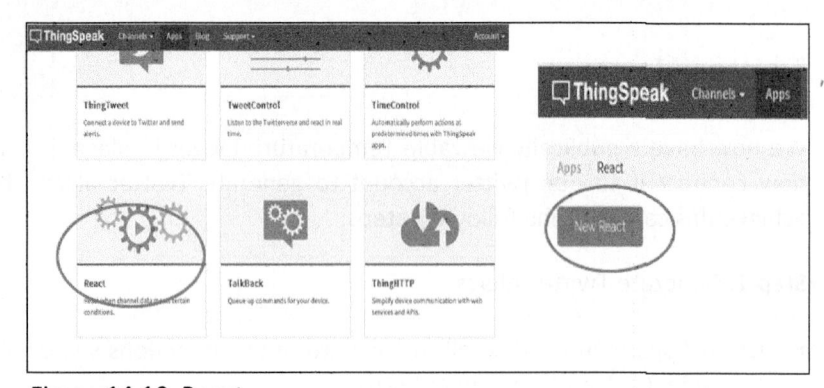

Figure 14.10 React

Step 3: Fill in React Details

- React Name: Enter a meaningful name,
- Condition Type: Since we are dealing with temperature values, select Numeric.
- Test Frequency: Choose suitable time interval, or set to every time the new data comes in.
- Condition: Temperature value to go above a specified value.
- Action: Since we wish to send a tweet select ThingTweet. Use your own Twitter account here.
- Select between "you want to tweet only the first time the condition is met" or "every time the condition is met".
- Click on "Save React". The sample React details are shown in Figure 14.11.

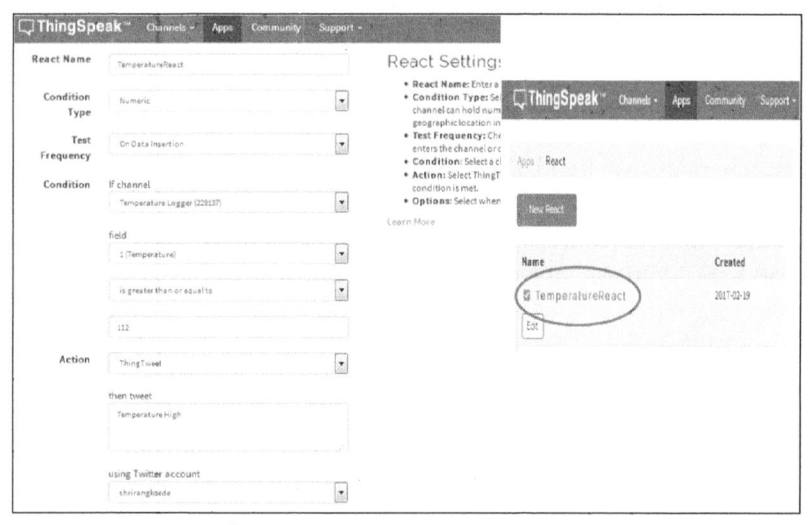

Experiment 14 : Public IoT based Temperature Logger **171**

Figure 14.11 Sample React

Step 4: Verify Tweets

Verify whether Tweets are generated on your Tweeter account. Verify its correctness against the Temperature logger graph from Channels | MyChannels.

Result

When the Arduino sketch is run, following things happen:

- Ready message is shown on the display monitor.
- AT commands are shown on the display monitor.
- IP address of ESP-8266 module is shown on the display monitor.
- The temperature values are shown on the display monitor.
- The temperature values are logged on to ThingSpeak channel.
- Tweets are generated as per setting done in the React.

Explanation

The **lm35Pin** is used to read temperature sensor values from A0 pin. The sketch relies on the Software Serial library. This library allows serial communication to take place on digital pins other than 0 and 1. The sketch uses "SoftwareSerial.h" for communication between Arduino and ESP-8266. Initially, object **esp8266** of **SoftwareSerial** is created, with pins as 2 and 3 as input to the constructor.

The **setup( )** function initializes serial communication with PC using **Serial.begin( )**. It also sets baud-rate for Software Serial port using **ser.begin( )**. The method **sendData( )** is used for configuring ESP-8266. Following steps are performed to configure ESP-8266 module before it can be used:

- Reset the ESP-8266 module using AT+RST command.

- Configure the ESP-8266 module to act as Access Point as well as station, using AT+CWMODE=3 command.

- Connect the ESP-8266 module to your Access Point using your SSID and password. The command is AT+CWJAP=<SSID>,<password>.

- Get the IP address of ESP-8266 module using AT+CIFSR command.

- Configure the ESP-8266 for single connection using command AT+CIPMUX=0.

In the **loop( )** function, the temperature readings are taken in a loop (10 readings) and an average value is calculated from these 10 readings. The temperature range and change of voltage per degree change are also considered while calculating the average temperature. This value is then converted to a string and sent to the ThingSpeak server. It is also printed on the display monitor. The statements that achieve this are shown below.

float temp = val * 50.0f / 1023.0f ;
String strTemp = String (temp, 1) ;
Serial.println (strTemp) ;

Experiment 14 : Public IoT based Temperature Logger

The TCP connection is established with the ThingSpeak server (api.thingspeak.com) at port 80 using the command "AT+CIPSTART". If an error occurs, it is shown on the display monitor through statements given below.

```
String cmd = "AT+CIPSTART=\"TCP\",\"" ;
cmd += "184.106.153.149" ; // api.thingspeak.com
cmd += "\",80" ;
ser.println ( cmd ) ;
if ( ser.find ( "Error" ) )
{
    Serial.println ( "AT+CIPSTART error" ) ;
    return ;
}
```

The GET string is prepared for sending temperature data to the ThingSpeak server using HTTP 1.1 protocol. The code that achieves this is shown below.

```
String getStr = "GET /update?api_key=" ;
getStr += apiKey ;
getStr +="&field1=" ;
getStr += String ( strTemp ) ;
getStr += "\r\n\r\n" ;
```

The "AT+CIPSEND" command and the length of the data are now sent. In the response from server, ">" is searched. If it is found, the string **getStr** is sent to the server. If ">" is not found, then it's an error and the connection with server is closed. This is shown below.

```
cmd = "AT+CIPSEND=" ;
cmd += String ( getStr.length ( ) ) ;
ser.println ( cmd ) ;

if ( esp8266.find ( ">" ) )
{
    ser.print ( getStr ) ;
}
else
{
    ser.println ( "AT+CIPCLOSE" ) ;
```

```
        Serial.println ( "AT+CIPCLOSE" ) ;
}
```

Functions Used

The functions used in this experiment are already covered in previous Experiments.

More Tweaks

Enhance the Experiment to use SD card and log the temperature data to the SD card.

EXPERIMENT FIFTEEN

INTERNET / INTRANET BASED HOME AUTOMATION

As technology advances, it reverses the characteristics of every situation again and again. The age of automation is going to be the age of 'do it yourself.

- Marshall McLuhan

Experiment

In the IoT scenario it is expected to control devices remotely over Internet / Intranet. This Experiment is about controlling electrical appliances like small pumps, light – bulb, fan over Internet / Intranet using a web interface. Since controlling using Internet requires a static IP address for the server, this Experiment demonstrates the same concept over Intranet.

Hardware Setup

This Experiment needs an ESP-8266 board, Application Board, Relay Board and Arduino Uno board. These are shown in Figures 15.1, 15.2, and 15.3.

Figure 15.1 ESP-8266 Board

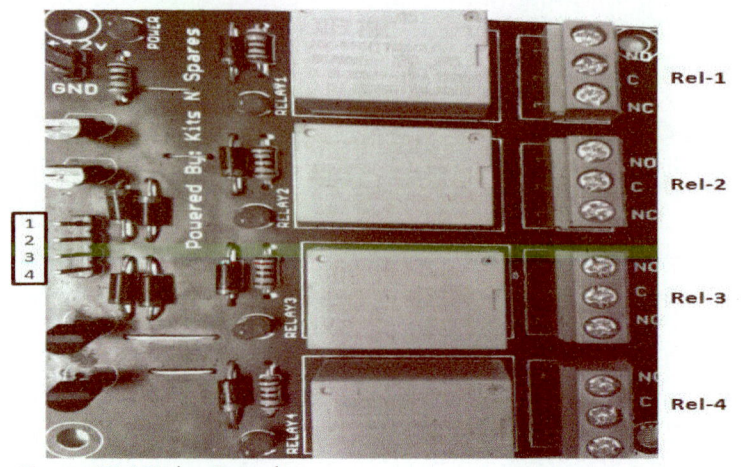

Figure 15.2 Relay Board

Experiment 15: Intranet based Home Automation

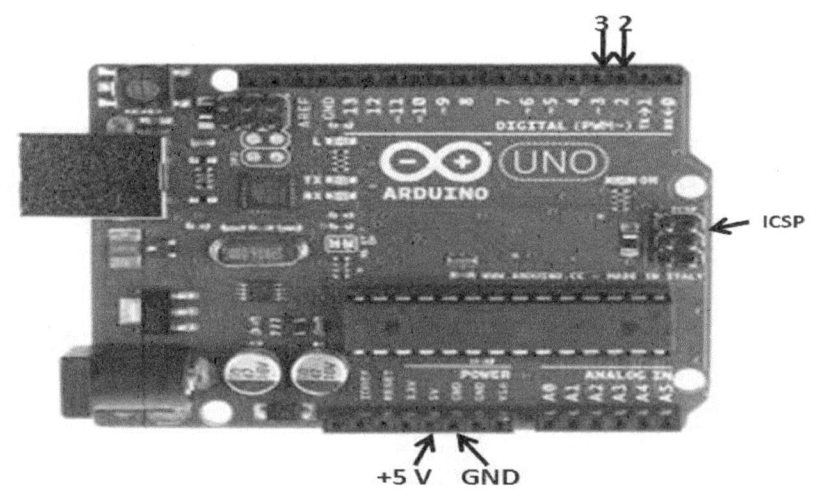

Figure 15.3 Arduino Uno

Pin connections shown in Figure 15.4 should be made.

Arduino Pins	Relay Board
Vin	+12V
GND	GND
Digital pin 10	4
Digital pin 11	3
Digital pin 12	2
Digital pin 13	1

Arduino Pins	ESP-8266 Board Pins
ICSP pin (+5V)	+5V
GND	GND
Digital pin 2	TX
Digital pin 3	RX

Figure 15.4 Pin connections

An appliance like bulb can be connected to a relay as shown in Figure 15.5.

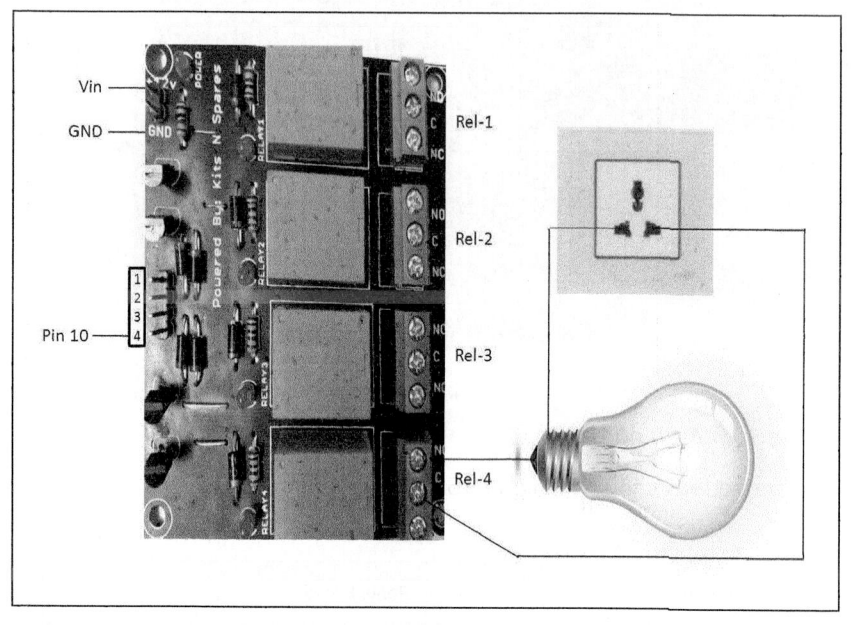

Figure 15.5 Connecting a bulb to a relay and AC mains power supply

Connect Power Adapter to the Arduino Uno board. Alternately, you can insert batteries in the battery holder and connect it to supply external power. Supplying external power is necessary, since the Relay board requires more voltage to drive relays.

Software Setup

Prepare a HTML page with four buttons. The page should also include a jquery library to handle button clicks. The library is used for sending HTTP requests to ESP-8266 module. Carry out the following steps as part of web page setup:

(1) Open notepad (/notepad++) editor and type in it the code given in the HTML Code section below. Save the file to some folder like

   D:\ Home_Automation\Home_Automation.html

Experiment 15: Intranet based Home Automation

(2) Download jquery library from https:// code.jquery.com/. A version jquery-1.1x.x.min.js serves the purpose. However, higher versions can also be tried.

(3) Copy the jquery library to the same folder

D:\ Home_Automation\jquery-1.1x.x.min.js

(4) Set the IP address of ESP-8266 module correctly in the HTML file. This is a very important step since the HTTP request is sent to this IP address.

HTML Code

```html
<html>
    <head>
        <title>Home Automation</title>
    </head>
    <body>

        <!-- in <button> tags ID attribute is the value sent to the arduino -->
        <button id="10" class="relay">Toggle Relay 1</button>
        <button id="11" class="relay">Toggle Relay 2</button>
        <button id="12" class="relay">Toggle Relay 3</button>
        <button id="13" class="relay">Toggle Relay 4</button>

        <script src="jquery-1.10.2.min.js"></script>
        <script type="text/javascript">
            $ ( document ).ready ( function( ) {
                $ ( ".relay" ).click ( function( ) {
                // get id value ( i.e. pin13, pin12, pin11, pin10 )
                    var p = $ ( this ).attr ( 'id' ) ;
            // send HTTP GET request to the IP address with the parameter
            // "pin" and value "p", then execute the function
            $.get ( "http:// 192.168.1.4:80/", {pin:p} ) ; // execute get req.
                });
            });
        </script>
    </body>
</html>
```

Sketch

```
// Home Automation
#include <SoftwareSerial.h>

#define DEBUG true

// connect pin 2 to TX of esp8266,
// connect pin 3 to RX of esp8266
SoftwareSerial esp8266 ( 2,3 ) ;

void setup( )
{
    Serial.begin ( 9600 ) ;
    esp8266.begin ( 9600 ) ;
    Serial.println ( "Ready!!" ) ;

    pinMode ( 10, OUTPUT ) ;
    digitalWrite ( 10, LOW ) ;

    pinMode ( 11, OUTPUT ) ;
    digitalWrite ( 11, LOW ) ;

    pinMode ( 12, OUTPUT ) ;
    digitalWrite ( 12, LOW ) ;

    pinMode ( 13, OUTPUT ) ;
    digitalWrite ( 13, LOW ) ;

    // reset module
    sendData ( "AT+RST\r\n", 2000, DEBUG ) ;
    // configure as access point as well as station
    sendData ( "AT+CWMODE=3\r\n", 1000, DEBUG ) ;
    // Connect to your access point, type your own SSID and password
    sendData ( "AT+CWJAP=\"UTkorde\", \"0123456789\"\r\n", 5000,
              DEBUG ) ;
    delay ( 3000 ) ;
    // get ip address
    sendData ( "AT+CIFSR\r\n", 3000, DEBUG ) ;
    delay ( 1000 ) ;
```

Experiment 15: Intranet based Home Automation

```
    // configure for multiple connections
    sendData ( "AT+CIPMUX=1\r\n", 2000, DEBUG ) ;
    // turn on server on port 80
    sendData ( "AT+CIPSERVER=1,80\r\n", 1000, DEBUG ) ;
}

void loop( )
{
    // check if the esp is sending a message
    if ( esp8266.available( ) )
    {
        if ( esp8266.find ( "+IPD," ) )
        {
            // wait for the serial buffer to fill up ( read all the serial data )
            delay ( 1000 ) ;
            // get the connection id so that we can then disconnect
            // subtract 48 because the read( ) function returns
            // ASCII value of is 48
            int connectionId = esp8266.read( ) - 48 ;

            // advance cursor to "pin="
            esp8266.find ( "pin=" ) ;

            // get first number
            int pinNumber = ( esp8266.read( ) - 48 ) * 10 ;
            // get second number,
            pinNumber += ( esp8266.read( ) - 48 ) ;

            // toggle pin
            digitalWrite ( pinNumber, !digitalRead ( pinNumber ) ) ;

            // make close command
            String closeCommand = "AT+CIPCLOSE=" ;
            // append connection id
            closeCommand += connectionId ;
            closeCommand += "\r\n" ;

            // close connection
            sendData ( closeCommand, 100, DEBUG ) ;
        }
    }
```

}

```
String sendData ( String command, const int timeout, boolean debug )
{
    String response = "" ;

    // send the read character to the esp8266

    esp8266.print ( command ) ;
    long int time = millis( ) ;

    while ( ( time + timeout ) > millis( ) )
    {
        while ( esp8266.available( ) )
        {
            // The esp has data so display its output to the serial window
            // read the next character
            char c = esp8266.read( ) ;
            response += c ;
        }
    }

    if ( debug )
    {
        Serial.print ( response ) ;
    }

    return response ;
}
```

Result

When the Arduino sketch is run, following things happen:

- Ready message is shown on the display monitor.

- AT commands are shown on the display monitor.

- IP address of ESP-8266 module is shown on the monitor.

Experiment 15: Intranet based Home Automation **183**

Toggle a button (e.g. Button 1). This should make the bulb off, if it is already glowing and vice-versa.

Open the HTML page in the browser. Make sure that IP address of ESP-8266 is correctly added to html script. Press the buttons in the HTML page. Watch the effect of toggling on the relay (i. e. bulb). Wait for a delay of few seconds.

Explanation

About html page

In the HTML page the **head** and **body** tags are defined. The **title** tag is used for specifying the title of the Experiment. In the **body** tag 4 buttons are defined with an id and an attribute class called **relay**. This part of the HTML script is given below.

```
<button id="10" class="relay">Toggle Relay 1</button>
<button id="11" class="relay">Toggle Relay 2</button>
<button id="12" class="relay">Toggle Relay 3</button>
<button id="13" class="relay">Toggle Relay 4</button>
```

The jquery library is included through the statement

```
<script src="jquery-1.10.2.min.js"></script>
```

The **click( )** function gets invoked when a button is pressed. The class attribute "relay" is used to have uniform response for various button clicks. This function uses the attribute "id" for deciding which button has been pressed and accordingly issues a HTTP GET request to the ESP-8266 module. This request is made by calling the **get( )** function. IP address and pin are sent as parameters to **get( )** function. The following part of the HTML script achieves this functionality:

```
$ ( ". relay " ).click ( function( ){
            var p = $ ( this ).attr ( 'id' ) ;
            $.get ( "http:// 192.168.1.4:80/", {pin:p} ) ;
       });
```

About Arduino sketch

The sketch relies on the Software Serial library. This library allows serial communication to take place on digital pins other than 0 and 1. The sketch uses "SoftwareSerial.h" for communication between Arduino and ESP-8266. Initially, object **esp8266** of SoftwareSerial is created, with pins as 2 and 3 as input to the constructor.

The **setup( )** function initializes serial communication with PC using **Serial.begin( )**. It also sets baud-rate for Software Serial port using **esp8266.begin( )**. The digital pins 10, 11, 12 and 13 are configured as OUTPUT using **pinMode( )** function. The **digitalWrite( )** functions sets these pins either HIGH or LOW. The method **sendData( )** is used for configuring ESP-8266. Following steps are performed to configure ESP-8266 module before it can be used:

- Reset the ESP-8266 module using AT+RST command.

- Configure the ESP-8266 module to act as Access Point as well as station, using AT+CWMODE=3 command.

- Connect the ESP-8266 module to your Access Point using your SSID and password. The command is AT+CWJAP=<SSID>,<password>.

- Get the IP of ESP-8266 module using AT+CIFSR command.

- Configure the ESP-8266 to have multiple connections. The command is AT+CIPMUX=1.

- Configure the ESP-8266 to act as server with port 80 being used for communication with client. The command is AT+CIPSERVER=1,80.

In the **loop( )** function, a check is performed whether ESP-8266 is sending any message. This can happen when a control command (via HTTP **get( )**) is received by ESP-8266 module. If the message is available then search for "+IPD," pattern is done. If this succeeds then read is performed to get connection Id. A variable **connnectionId** is used to store the value after subtraction of 48 to get the decimal number. Then reading is advanced to find "pin=" pattern. The following code gives this:

```
if ( esp8266.find ( "+IPD," ) )
{
```

Experiment 15: Intranet based Home Automation

```
    delay ( 1000 ) ;
    int connectionId = esp8266.read( ) - 48 ;
    esp8266.find ( "pin=" ) ;
    ...
}
```

The pin number is read in the variable **pinNumber**. This is done in two steps. Firstly, most significant digit is read and is multiplied by 10 to get ten's digit. This is followed by reading unit place's digit and sum is performed to get the actual pin number. After this, the pin is toggled using **digitalWrite( )** function which results in corresponding device (like bulb) to get toggled. This is achieved through the code given below.

```
int pinNumber = ( esp8266.read( ) - 48 ) * 10 ;
pinNumber += ( esp8266.read( ) - 48 ) ;
digitalWrite ( pinNumber, !digitalRead ( pinNumber ) ) ;
```

Finally, the connection is closed by issuing close command using **connectionId**.

Functions Used

The functions used in this experiment are explained in Experiment 13.

More Tweaks

Develop a Arduino sketch and HTML page with javascript code to control other appliances like fan or a small pump.

EXPERIMENT SIXTEEN

STREET LIGHT CONTROL

If you look at landscape in historical terms, you realize that most of the time we have been on Earth as a species, what has fallen on our retina is landscape, not images of buildings and cars and street lights.

- Bill Viola

Experiment

This Experiment is about controlling a street light (or a porch bulb) based on the current light intensity. The status of the bulb is updated on Internet, so that it can be viewed from anywhere in the world.

Hardware Setup

This Experiment needs an ESP-8266 board, Application Board, Relay Board, Application board and Arduino Uno board. These are shown in Figures 16.1, 16.2, and 16.3.

Figure 16.1 ESP-8266 Board

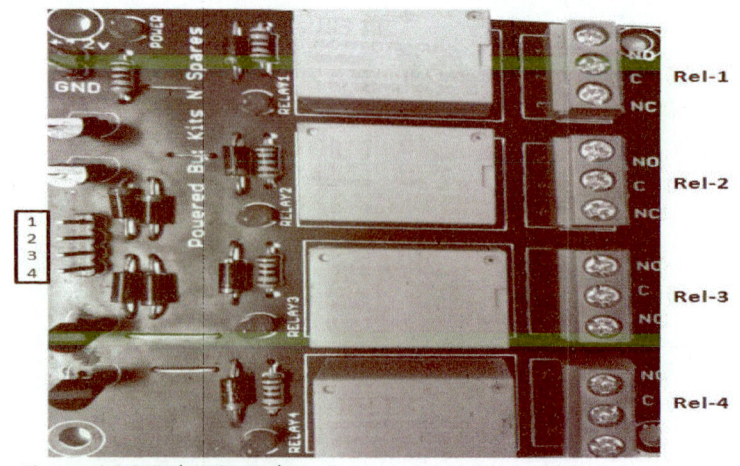

Figure 16.2 Relay Board

Experiment 16: Street Light Control **189**

Figure 16.3 Application Board

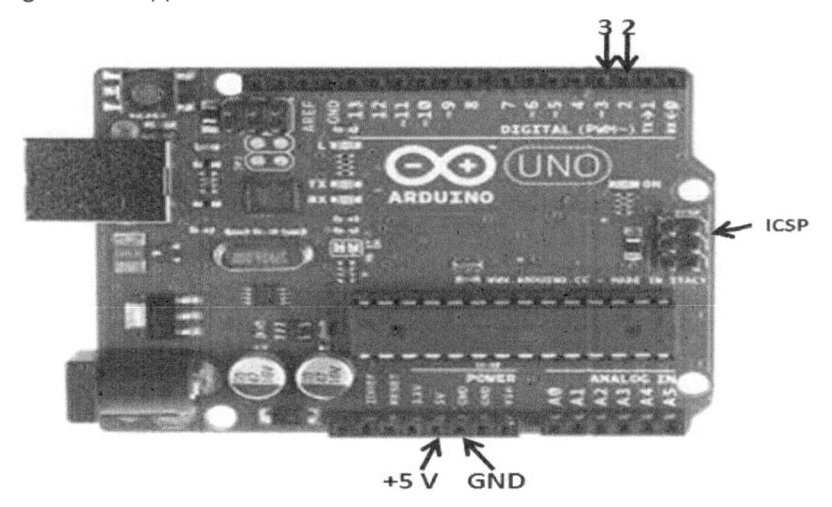

Figure 16.4 Arduino Uno

Pin connections shown in Figure 16.5 should be made.

Arduino Pins	ESP-8266 Board Pins
Digital pin 2	TX
Digital pin 3	RX

Arduino Pins	Application Board Pins
+5V	+5 V
GND	GND
A0	LDR

Application Board Pins	ESP-8266 Board Pins
+5V	+5V
GND	GND

Arduino Pins	Relay Board Pins
Vin	+12 V
GND	GND
Digital pin 10	4

Figure 16.5 Pin connections

An appliance like bulb should be connected to a relay as shown in Figure 16.6.

Experiment 16: Street Light Control **191**

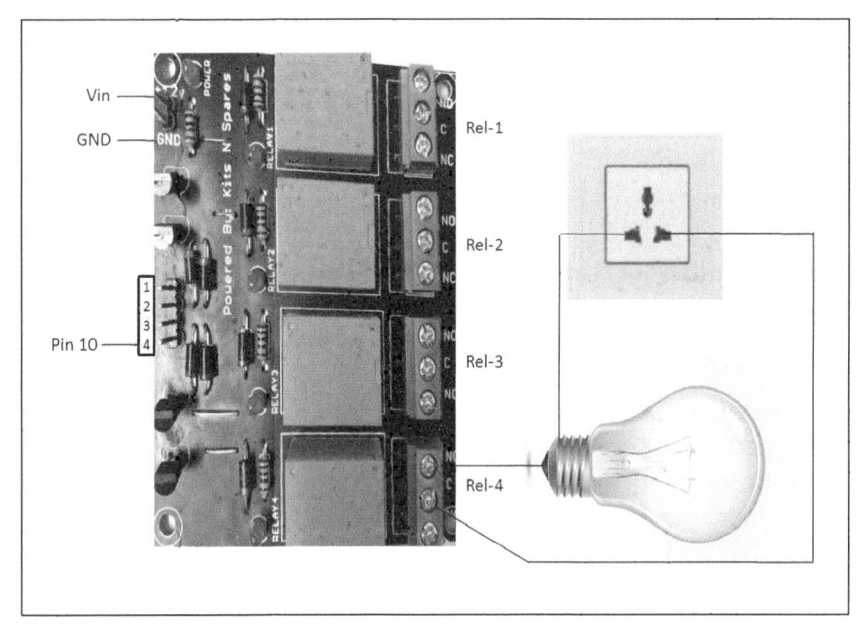

Figure 16.6 Connecting a Porch bulb

Connect Power Adapter to the Arduino Uno board. Alternately, you can insert batteries in the battery holder and connect it to supply external power. Supplying external power is necessary, since the Relay board requires more voltage to drive relays.

Software Setup

To perform the Experiment following steps should be carried out:

1. Setup ThingSpeak and Create a new channel. Refer "Internet Based Temperature Logger" in Experiment 14 for details of this step.
2. Develop Arduino sketch and execute it.

Sketch

```
// Street light control with status logging to Internet

#include <SoftwareSerial.h>
#include <stdlib.h>
```

```
#define DEBUG true
// LED
int ledPin = 13 ;

int LDR_pin = A0 ;
int relay_Pin=10 ;

// replace with your channel's thingspeak API key,
// API key should be different for every expt., i.e. for every channel
String apiKey = "DA3VAFP71KVPLRHP" ;

// connect 2 to TX of Serial USB
// connect 3 to RX of serial USB
SoftwareSerial ser ( 2, 3 ) ; // RX, TX

// this runs once
void setup( )
{
    // initialize the digital pin as an output
    pinMode ( ledPin, OUTPUT ) ;
    pinMode ( relay_Pin, OUTPUT ) ;
    // enable debug serial
    Serial.begin ( 9600 ) ;
    // enable software serial
    ser.begin ( 9600 ) ;

    // reset ESP8266
    sendData ( "AT+RST\r\n", 2000, DEBUG ) ;
    // configure as access point as well as station
    sendData ( "AT+CWMODE=3\r\n", 1000, DEBUG ) ;
    // Connect to your access point, type your own SSID and password
    sendData ( "AT+CWJAP=\"UTkorde\", \"XXXXXXXXXX\"\r\n", 5000,
            DEBUG ) ;
    delay ( 3000 ) ;
    sendData ( "AT+CIFSR\r\n", 3000, DEBUG ) ; // get ip address
    delay ( 1000 ) ;
}

int temp = 0 ;

void loop( )
```

Experiment 16: Street Light Control

```
{
    // blink LED on board
    digitalWrite ( ledPin, HIGH ) ;
    delay ( 200 ) ;
    digitalWrite ( ledPin, LOW ) ;

    // 512, detect when light intensity low
    if ( analogRead ( LDR_pin ) < 512 )
    {
        // turn on the relay
        digitalWrite ( relay_Pin, HIGH ) ;
        // feed temp variable with 1 to indicate relay is ON
        temp = 1 ;
    }
    // 512 detect when light intensity HIGH
    if ( analogRead ( LDR_pin ) > 512 )
    {
        // turn off the relay
        digitalWrite ( relay_Pin, LOW ) ;
        // feed temp variable with 0 to indicate relay is OFF
        temp = 0 ;
    }
    // magnify, adjust the multiplication factor
    // so that thingspeak graph can show the value
    temp = temp * 100 ;
    if ( temp == 0 )
    {
        // temp is set to 50 so that value
        // is visible in thingspeak graph
        temp = 50 ;
    }
    // convert to string
    String strTemp = String ( temp, 1 ) ;
    Serial.println ( strTemp ) ;

    // TCP connection
    String cmd = "AT+CIPSTART=\"TCP\",\"" ;
    cmd += "184.106.153.149" ; // api.thingspeak.com
    cmd += "\",80" ;
    ser.println ( cmd ) ;
```

```
    if ( ser.find ( "Error" ) )
    {
        Serial.println ( "AT+CIPSTART error" ) ;
        return ;
    }

    // prepare GET string
    String getStr = "GET /update?api_key=" ;
    getStr += apiKey ;
    getStr += "&field1=" ;
    getStr += String ( strTemp ) ;
    getStr += "\r\n\r\n" ;

    // send data length
    cmd = "AT+CIPSEND=" ;
    cmd += String ( getStr.length( ) ) ;
    ser.println ( cmd ) ;

    if ( ser.find ( ">" ) )
    {
        ser.print ( getStr ) ;
    }
    else
    {
        ser.println ( "AT+CIPCLOSE" ) ;
        // alert user
        Serial.println ( "AT+CIPCLOSE" ) ;
    }
    // thingspeak needs 15 sec delay between updates
    delay ( 16000 ) ;
}

String sendData ( String command, const int timeout, boolean debug )
{
    String response = "" ;
    // send the read character to the esp8266
    ser.print ( command ) ;
    long int time = millis( ) ;

    while ( ( time + timeout ) > millis( ) )
```

Experiment 16: Street Light Control

```
    {
        while ( ser.available( ) )
        {
            // read the next character
            char c = ser.read( ) ;
            response += c ;
        }
    }

    if ( debug )
    {
        Serial.print ( response ) ;
    }

    return response ;
}
```

Result

When the Arduino sketch is run, following things happen:

- Ready message is shown on the display monitor.

- AT commands are shown on the display monitor.

- IP address of ESP-8266 module is shown on the display monitor.

- Put some light (using a torch) on the LDR and see the effect. Take the torch away from the LDR and see the effect.

- The toggling of status of Relay (or bulb) is logged to the ThingSpeak channel.

Explanation

The sketch relies on the Software Serial library. This library allows serial communication to take place on digital pins other than 0 and 1. The sketch uses "SoftwareSerial.h" for communication between Arduino and

ESP-8266. Initially, object **esp8266** of SoftwareSerial is created, with pins as 2 and 3 as input to the constructor.

The **setup( )** function initializes serial communication with PC using **Serial.begin( )**. It also sets baud-rate for Software Serial port using **esp8266.begin( )**. The digital pin 10 is configured as OUTPUT using **pinMode( )** function. The method **sendData( )** is used for configuring ESP-8266. Following steps are performed to configure ESP-8266 module before it can be used:

- Reset the ESP-8266 module using AT+RST command.
- Configure the ESP-8266 module to act as Access Point as well as station using AT+CWMODE=3 command.
- Connect the ESP-8266 module to your Access Point using the command AT+CWJAP=<SSID>,<password>.
- Get the IP address of ESP-8266 module using AT+CIFSR command.
- Configure ESP-8266 module for multiple connections using AT+CIPMUX=1 command.

In the **loop( )** function, the light intensity is detected by reading LDR value at analog pin denoted by **LDR_pin**. The function **analogRead( )** is used to read the value. A threshold of 512 is used (which can be adjusted as per requirement) to decide whether to make the relay ON or OFF. The relay is controlled using the function **digitalWrite( )**. A variable **temp** is used to indicate the status of relay. This value is magnified 100 times so that when logged to ThingSpeak it is visible on the graph. The code that achieves this is shown below:

```
if ( analogRead ( LDR_pin ) < 512 )
{
    digitalWrite ( relay_Pin, HIGH ) ;
    temp = 1 ;
}

if ( analogRead ( LDR_pin ) > 512 )
{
    digitalWrite ( relay_Pin, LOW ) ;
    temp = 0 ;
}
```

Experiment 16: Street Light Control **197**

```
temp = temp * 100 ;
if ( temp == 0 )
{
    temp = 50 ; // to make it visible in graph
}
```

The TCP connection is established with the ThingSpeak server (api.thingspeak.com) at port 80 using the command "AT+CIPSTART". If an error occurs, it is shown on the display monitor using the following code:

```
String cmd = "AT+CIPSTART=\"TCP\",\"" ;
cmd += "184.106.153.149" ; // api.thingspeak.com
cmd += "\",80" ;
ser.println ( cmd ) ;

if ( ser.find ( "Error" ) )
{
    Serial.println ( "AT+CIPSTART error" ) ;
    return ;
}
```

The GET string is prepared for sending temperature data to the ThingSpeak server using HTTP 1.1 protocol. The code that achieves this is shown below.

```
String getStr = "GET /update?api_key=" ;
getStr += apiKey ;
getStr +="&field1=" ;
getStr += String ( strTemp ) ;
getStr += "\r\n\r\n" ;
```

The "AT+CIPSEND" command and the length of the data are now sent to the server. In the response from server, ">" is searched. If it is found, the string **getStr** is sent to the server. If ">" is not found, then it's an error and the connection with the server is closed. This is shown below.

```
cmd = "AT+CIPSEND=" ;
cmd += String ( getStr.length( ) ) ;
ser.println ( cmd ) ;
```

```
if ( esp8266.find ( ">" ) )
{
    ser.print ( getStr ) ;
}
else
{
    ser.println ( "AT+CIPCLOSE" ) ;
    Serial.println ( "AT+CIPCLOSE" ) ;
}
```

Functions Used

The functions used in this experiment are already explained in previous Experiments.

More Tweaks

Enhance the experiment to send tweets when the street light / porch light is switched ON and OFF.

EXPERIMENT SEVENTEEN

HOME SECURITY SYSTEM

Home is where children find safety and security, where we find our identities, where citizenship starts. It usually starts with believing you're part of a community, and that is essential to having a stable home.

- Matthew Desmond

Experiment

This Experiment is to detect a presence of on intruder within a specified area of the home (like courtyard). A sound alarm gets raised when an object is within the predefined range. Continuous monitoring is also provided by logging the measurements to ThingSpeak. It can also be linked it with social networking platform, Twitter. This allows receiving tweets for the user-defined conditions, like, suspicious object detection.

Hardware Setup

This Experiment needs an ESP-8266 board, Application Board, Ultrasonic sensor, and Arduino Uno board. These are shown in Figures 17.1, 17.2 17.3 and 17.4.

Figure 17.1 ESP-8266 Board

Experiment 17: Home Security System   **201**

Figure 17.2 Application Board

Figure 17.3 Ultrasonic sensor

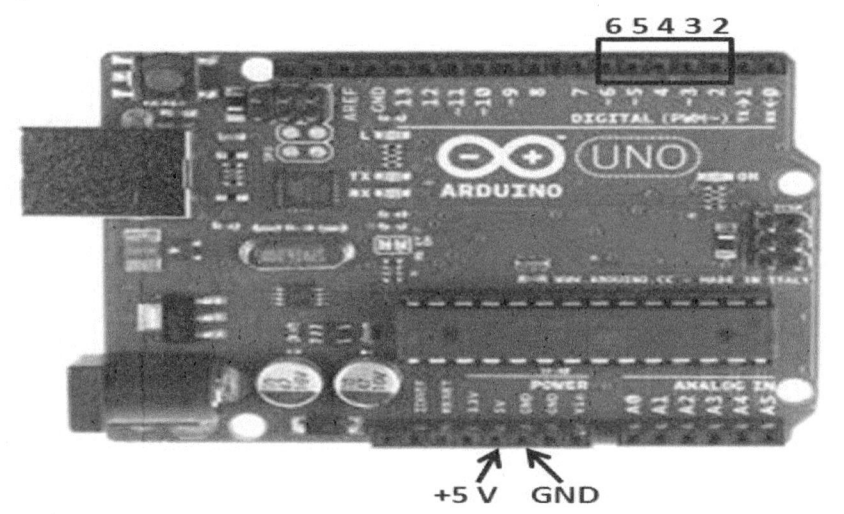

Figure 17.4 Arduino Uno

Pin connections shown in Figure 17.5 should be made.

Arduino Pins	ESP-8266 Board Pins
Digital pin 2	TX
Digital pin 3	RX

Arduino Pins	Application Board Pins
+5V	+5 V
GND	GND
Digital pin 6	BUZ

Application Board Pins	ESP-8266 Board Pins
+5V	+5V
GND	GND

Arduino Pins	Ultrasonic Sensor
Digital pin 4	Echo
Digital pin 5	Trig

Applicaton Board Pins	Ultrasonic Sensor
+5V	+5V
GND	GND

Figure 17.5 Pin connections

Experiment 17: Home Security System

Connect Power Adapter to the Arduino Uno board (or insert batteries in the battery holder and connect). Switch it ON so that external supply is provided.

Software Setup

To perform this Experiment, carry out the following steps:

1. Setup ThingSpeak and create a new Channel called "DistanceMeasurment" and a React called "DistanceReact".
2. Configure ThingSpeak to link it to Twitter account. Refer "Internet Based Temperature Logger" discussed in Experiment 14, for details of ThingSpeak setup.
3. We also need to setup the Ultrasonic sensor library. To do this first Download "NewPing" library from the link

   https:// bitbucket.org/teckel12/arduino-new-ping/downloads/
4. Download either NewPing_v1.7.zip or NewPing_v1.8.zip and copy the zip file to folder "C:\library\".
5. Go to Arduino IDE | Sketch | Include Library | Add .ZIP library. Select NewPing_v1.7.zip.
6. Develop Arduino Sketch and execute it.

Sketch

```
// Home Security
#include <SoftwareSerial.h>
#include <stdlib.h>
#include <NewPing.h>
#define DEBUG true

#define TRIGGER_PIN 5
#define ECHO_PIN 4
#define MAX_DISTANCE 300

// LED
int ledPin = 13 ;
```

```c
// Buzzer Pin
int Buzzer = 6 ;

NewPing uSensor ( TRIGGER_PIN, ECHO_PIN, MAX_DISTANCE ) ;

// replace with your channel's thingspeak API key
String apiKey = "08XG14R457CYLNYA" ;

// connect 2 to TX of Serial USB
// connect 3 to RX of serial USB
SoftwareSerial ser ( 2, 3 ) ; // RX, TX

void setup( )
{
    // initialize the digital pin as an output
    pinMode ( ledPin, OUTPUT ) ;
    pinMode ( Buzzer, OUTPUT ) ;

    // enable debug serial
    Serial.begin ( 9600 ) ;
    // enable software serial
    ser.begin ( 9600 ) ;

    // reset ESP8266
    sendData ( "AT+RST\r\n", 2000, DEBUG ) ;
    // configure as access point as well as station
    sendData ( "AT+CWMODE=3\r\n", 1000, DEBUG ) ;
    // Connect to your access point, type your own SSID and password
    sendData ( "AT+CWJAP=\"UTkorde\", \"XXXXXXXXX\"\r\n", 5000,
            DEBUG ) ;
    delay ( 3000 ) ;
    // get ip address
    sendData ( "AT+CIFSR\r\n", 3000, DEBUG ) ;
    delay ( 1000 ) ;
    // single connection
    sendData ( "AT+CIPMUX=0\r\n", 2000, DEBUG ) ;
}

void loop( )
{
    // blink LED on board
```

Experiment 17: Home Security System

```
digitalWrite ( ledPin, HIGH ) ;
delay ( 200 ) ;
digitalWrite ( ledPin, LOW ) ;

// read the value from ultrasonic sensor
// read 10 values for averaging.
float val = 0.0 ;
for ( int i = 0 ; i < 10 ; i++ )
{
    // get distance from ultrasonic sensor
    unsigned int ultraSen = uSensor.ping( ) ;
    val = val + ( float ) ultraSen / ( float ) US_ROUNDTRIP_CM ;
    delay ( 500 ) ;
}

// take average
val = val / 10 ;

// magnify as per need
val = val * 10 ;
// make buzzer high if the value of distance is lower than cutoff
if ( val < 120 ) // 120 cm
{
    digitalWrite ( Buzzer, HIGH ) ;
}

// make buzzer low if the value of distance is greater than cutoff
if ( val > 120 )
{
    digitalWrite ( Buzzer, LOW ) ;
}

float temp = val ;
// convert to string
String strTemp = String ( temp, 1 ) ;
Serial.println ( strTemp ) ;

// TCP connection
String cmd = "AT+CIPSTART=\"TCP\",\"" ;
cmd += "184.106.153.149" ; // api.thingspeak.com
cmd += "\",80" ;
```

```
    ser.println ( cmd ) ;

    if ( ser.find ( "Error" ) )
    {
        Serial.println ( "AT+CIPSTART error" ) ;
        return ;
    }

    // prepare GET string
    String getStr = "GET /update?api_key=" ;
    getStr += apiKey ;
    getStr += "&field1=" ;
    getStr += String ( strTemp ) ;
    getStr += "\r\n\r\n" ;

    // send data length
    cmd = "AT+CIPSEND=" ;
    cmd += String ( getStr.length( ) ) ;
    ser.println ( cmd ) ;

    if ( ser.find ( ">" ) )
    {
        ser.print ( getStr ) ;
    }
    else
    {
        ser.println ( "AT+CIPCLOSE" ) ;
        // alert user
        Serial.println ( "AT+CIPCLOSE" ) ;
    }

    // thingspeak needs 15 sec delay between updates
    delay ( 16000 ) ;
}

String sendData ( String command, const int timeout, boolean debug )
{
    String response = "" ;
    // send the read character to the esp8266
    ser.print ( command ) ;
    long int time = millis( ) ;
```

Experiment 17: Home Security System

```
    while ( ( time + timeout ) > millis( ) )
    {
        while ( ser.available( ) )
        {
            // read the next character
            char c = ser.read( ) ;
            response += c ;
        }
    }

    if ( debug )
    {
        Serial.print ( response ) ;
    }

    return response ;
}
```

Result

When the Arduino sketch is run, following things happen:

- Ready message is shown on the display monitor.

- AT commands are shown on the display monitor.

- IP address of ESP-8266 module is shown on the display monitor.

- The distance values are shown on the display monitor.

- Bring an object close to ultrasonic sensor so that a sound from buzzer is heard and then take it away. When the object is gone the buzzer sound stops.

- The distance values are logged on to ThingSpeak channel.

- Tweets are generated as per setting done in the ThingReact.

Explanation

The ultrasonic sensor is used to read the distance between sensor and object. The ultrasonic sensor's Trigger (called Trig) pin and Echo pin are used. These pins are connected to Digital pin 5 and Digital pin 4 of Arduino. The library "**NewPing.h**" is required for working of the sensor. The object **uSensor** requires pins 5 and 4 as constructor parameters.

The sketch relies on the Software Serial library. This library allows serial communication to take place on digital pins other than 0 and 1. The sketch uses "**SoftwareSerial.h**" for communication between Arduino and ESP-8266. Initially, object **ser** of SoftwareSerial is created, with pins 2 and 3 as input to the constructor.

The **setup( )** function initializes serial communication with PC using **Serial.begin( )**. It also sets baud-rate for Software Serial port using **ser.begin( )**. The buzzer pin is configured as OUTPUT using the function **digitalWrite( )**. The method **sendData( )** is used for configuring ESP-8266. Following steps are performed to configure ESP-8266 module before it can be used:

- Reset the ESP-8266 module using AT+RST command.
- Configure the ESP-8266 module to act as Access Point as well as station using AT+CWMODE=3 command.
- Connect the ESP-8266 module to your Access Point using the command AT+CWJAP=<SSID>,<password>.
- Get the IP of ESP-8266 module using AT+CIFSR command.
- Configure ESP-8266 module for single connection using AT+CIPMUX=0 command.

In the **loop( )** function, 10 ultrasonic readings are taken in a loop. From these values an average value is calculated. The function **uSensor.ping( )** is used to obtain distance of an object from the sensor. This method is part of **NewPing** library. The ping value is divided by a macro US_ROUNDTRIP_CM defined in "**NewPing.h**". This is achieved through the code given below.

```
for ( int i = 0 ; i < 10 ; i++ )
```

Experiment 17: Home Security System

```
{
    unsigned int ultraSen = uSensor.ping( ) ;
    val = val + ( float ) ultraSen / ( float ) US_ROUNDTRIP_CM ;
    delay ( 500 ) ;
}
```

Magnification of average value is done so that the values logged at ThingSpeak are visible in a graph. The magnification is based on the application's need. User is free to choose an appropriate magnification value.

A cutoff value for distance is used to sound an alarm via buzzer. When an object is within the cutoff distance, the buzzer will make sound, otherwise, it will not. This is shown in the following code:

```
val = val / 10 ;
val = val * 10 ;
if ( val < 120 )
{
    digitalWrite ( Buzzer, HIGH ) ;
}
if ( val > 120 )
{
    digitalWrite ( Buzzer,LOW ) ;
}
```

The distance value is to be sent to ThingSpeak. Hence it is converted into a string. It is also printed on the display monitor.

The TCP connection is established with the ThingSpeak server (api.thingspeak.com) at port 80 using the command "AT+CIPSTART". If an error occurs, it is shown on the display monitor using the following code:

```
String cmd = "AT+CIPSTART=\"TCP\",\"" ;
cmd += "184.106.153.149" ; // api.thingspeak.com
cmd += "\",80" ;
ser.println ( cmd ) ;
if ( ser.find ( "Error" ) )
{
    Serial.println ( "AT+CIPSTART error" ) ;
    return ;
```

}

The GET string is prepared for sending temperature data to the ThingSpeak server using HTTP 1.1 protocol. The code that achieves this is shown below.

```
String getStr = "GET /update?api_key=" ;
getStr += apiKey ;
getStr +="&field1=" ;
getStr += String ( strTemp ) ;
getStr += "\r\n\r\n" ;
```

The "AT+CIPSEND" command and the length of the data are now sent to the server. In the response from server, ">" is searched. If it is found, the string **getStr** is sent to the server. If ">" is not found, then it's an error and the connection with server is closed. This is shown below:

```
cmd = "AT+CIPSEND=" ;
cmd += String ( getStr.length( ) ) ;
ser.println ( cmd ) ;
if ( esp8266.find ( ">" ) )
{
    ser.print ( getStr ) ;
}
else
{
    ser.println ( "AT+CIPCLOSE" ) ;
    Serial.println ( "AT+CIPCLOSE" ) ;
}
```

Functions Used

The functions used in this experiment are already covered in previous Experiments.

More Tweaks

Adapt the Experiment for managing parking system of an apartment. Ensure that a wireless point is available in the parking system.

EXPERIMENT
EIGHTEEN

WATER LEVEL MONITOR

Water is the driving force of all nature.

- Leonardo da Vici

Experiment

This Experiment is to monitor the water level in a water container/tank. on a continuous basis. The water level measurements are also logged to ThingSpeak so that they can be monitored over Internet/Intranet. Provision should also be made to link the measurements with social networking platform, Twitter. This permits receiving tweets by the user under conditions like high water level.

Hardware Setup

This Experiment needs an ESP-8266 board, Arduino Uno board Application Board and Probes/Wire connectors. These are shown in Figures 18.1, 18.2 and 18.3.

Figure 18.1 ESP-8266 Board

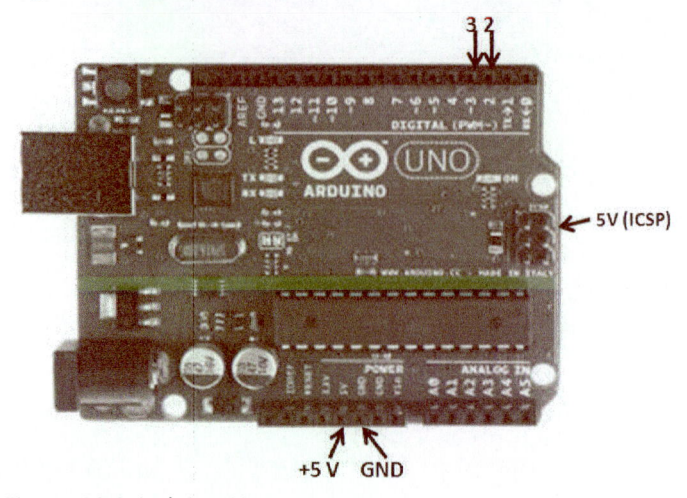

Figure 18.2 Arduino Uno

Experiment 18: Water Level Monitor **213**

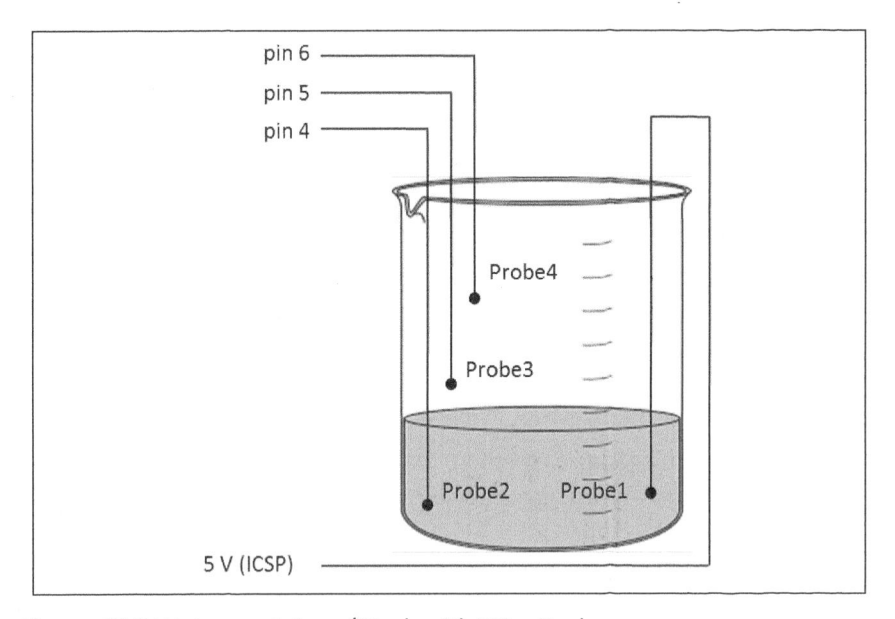

```
                    pin 6 ─────────┐
                    pin 5 ──────┐  │
                    pin 4 ───┐  │  │
```

Figure 18.3 Water container / Tank with Wire Probes

Pin connections shown in Figure 18.4 should be made.

Arduino Pins	ESP-8266 Board Pins
Digital pin 2	TX
Digital pin 3	RX
+5V	+5V
GND	GND

Arduino Pins	Probes (Water Container)
5V (ICSP pin)	Probe1
Digital pin 4	Probe2
Digital pin 5	Probe3
Digital pin 6	Probe4

Figure 18.4 Pin connections

Connect Power Adapter to the Arduino Uno board. Alternately, you can insert batteries in the battery holder and connect it to supply external power.

Software Setup

To perform this Experiment, carry out the following steps:

1. Setup ThingSpeak and create a new Channel called "LevelMeasurment" and a React called "LevelReact".
2. Configure ThingSpeak to link it to Twitter account. Refer "Internet Based Temperature Logger" discussed in Experiment 14, for details of ThingSpeak setup.
3. Develop Arduino Sketch and execute it.

Sketch

```
// Water level monitor
#include <SoftwareSerial.h>
#include <stdlib.h>
#define DEBUG true

// LED
int ledPin = 13 ;
// define input pins
int high_level = 6 ;
int med_level= 5 ;
int low_level= 4 ;

// replace with your channel's thingspeak API key
String apiKey = "Z601MBRIWPRV2Z4H" ;

// connect 2 to TX of Serial USB
// connect 3 to RX of serial USB
SoftwareSerial ser ( 2, 3 ) ; // RX, TX

// this runs once
```

Experiment 18: Water Level Monitor

```
void setup( )
{
    // initialize the digital pin as an output.
    pinMode ( ledPin, OUTPUT ) ;

    pinMode ( high_level, INPUT ) ;
    pinMode ( med_level, INPUT ) ;
    pinMode ( low_level, INPUT ) ;

    digitalWrite ( high_level, LOW ) ;
    digitalWrite ( med_level, LOW ) ;
    digitalWrite ( low_level, LOW ) ;

    // enable debug serial
    Serial.begin ( 9600 ) ;
    // enable software serial
    ser.begin ( 9600 ) ;

    // reset ESP8266
    sendData ( "AT+RST\r\n", 2000, DEBUG ) ;
    // configure as access point as well as station
    sendData ( "AT+CWMODE=3\r\n", 1000, DEBUG ) ;
    // Connect to your access point, type your own SSID and password
    sendData ( "AT+CWJAP=\"UTkorde\", \"0123456789\"\r\n", 5000,
               DEBUG ) ;
    delay ( 3000 ) ;
    // get ip address
    sendData ( "AT+CIFSR\r\n", 3000, DEBUG ) ;
    delay ( 1000 ) ;
    // single connection
    sendData ( "AT+CIPMUX=0\r\n", 2000, DEBUG ) ;
}

int level = 0 ;

void loop( )
{
    // blink LED on board
    digitalWrite ( ledPin, HIGH ) ;
    delay ( 200 ) ;
    digitalWrite ( ledPin, LOW ) ;
```

```
if ( digitalRead ( high_level ) == LOW && digitalRead ( med_level ) ==
    LOW && digitalRead ( low_level ) == LOW )
{
    level = 0 ;
}

if ( digitalRead ( high_level ) == LOW && digitalRead ( med_level ) ==
    LOW && digitalRead ( low_level ) == HIGH )
{
    level = 1 ;
}

if ( digitalRead ( high_level ) == LOW && digitalRead ( med_level ) ==
    HIGH && digitalRead ( low_level ) == HIGH )
{
    level = 2 ;
}

if ( digitalRead ( high_level ) == HIGH && digitalRead ( med_level ) ==
    HIGH && digitalRead ( low_level ) == HIGH )
{
    level = 3 ;
}

// magnify the number as just 0,1,2,3 is not good to get plotted
level = level * 10 ;

// convert to string
String strTemp = String ( level ) ;
Serial.println ( strTemp ) ;

// TCP connection
String cmd = "AT+CIPSTART=\"TCP\",\"" ;
cmd += "184.106.153.149" ; // api.thingspeak.com
cmd += "\",80" ;
ser.println ( cmd ) ;

if ( ser.find ( "Error" ) )
{
    Serial.println ( "AT+CIPSTART error" ) ;
```

Experiment 18: Water Level Monitor   **217**

```
        return ;
    }

    // prepare GET string
    String getStr = "GET /update?api_key=" ;
    getStr += apiKey ;
    getStr +="&field1=" ;
    getStr += String ( strTemp ) ;
    getStr += "\r\n\r\n" ;

    // send data length
    cmd = "AT+CIPSEND=" ;
    cmd += String ( getStr.length( ) ) ;
    ser.println ( cmd ) ;

    if ( ser.find ( ">" ) )
    {
        ser.print ( getStr ) ;
    }
    else
    {
        ser.println ( "AT+CIPCLOSE" ) ;
        // alert user
        Serial.println ( "AT+CIPCLOSE" ) ;
    }

    // thingspeak needs 15 sec delay between updates
    delay ( 16000 ) ;
}

String sendData ( String command, const int timeout, boolean debug )
{
    String response = "" ;
    // send the read character to the esp8266
    ser.print ( command ) ;
    long int time = millis( ) ;

    while ( ( time + timeout ) > millis( ) )
    {
        while ( ser.available( ) )
        {
```

```
            // read the next character
            char c = ser.read( ) ;
            response += c ;
        }
    }

    if ( debug )
    {
        Serial.print ( response ) ;
    }

    return response ;
}
```

Result

When the Arduino sketch is run, following things happen:

- Ready message is shown on the display monitor.

- AT commands are shown on the display monitor.

- IP address of ESP-8266 module is shown on the monitor.

- The water level values are shown on the display monitor.

- Pour the water in the container (or remove the water). Add little salt to make water salty for current conduction.

- The water level values are logged to ThingSpeak channel.

- Tweets are generated as per setting done in ThingReact.

Explanation

The sketch makes use of the basic concept that current flows through salty water. +5V terminal is dipped at one end of the tank and other three probes are dipped at other end of the container. These probes are

Experiment 18: Water Level Monitor **219**

placed at different levels to monitor the water level. Three Digital pins are used to monitor high level, medium level and low level.

The sketch relies on the Software Serial library. This library allows serial communication to take place on digital pins other than 0 and 1. The sketch uses "**SoftwareSerial.h**" for communication between Arduino and ESP-8266. Initially, object **ser** of SoftwareSerial is created with pins 2 and 3 as input to the constructor.

The **setup( )** configures the digital pins used for measuring level as INPUT. These pins are set to LOW, so that when water reaches these pins, current conduction can happen. This function also initializes serial communication with PC using **Serial.begin( )**. It also sets baud-rate for Software Serial port using **ser.begin( )**. The buzzer pin is configured as OUTPUT using **digitalWrite( )**. The method **sendData( )** is used for configuring ESP-8266. Following steps are performed to configure ESP-8266 module before it can be used:

- Reset the ESP-8266 module using AT+RST command.
- Configure the ESP-8266 module to act as Access Point as well as station using AT+CWMODE=3 command.
- Connect the ESP-8266 module to your Access Point using the command AT+CWJAP=<SSID>,<password>.
- Get the IP of ESP-8266 module using AT+CIFSR command.
- Configure ESP-8266 module for single connection using AT+CIPMUX=0 command.

In the **loop( )** function, the digital pins connected to probes are read using the **digitalRead( )** function. The values for three levels are checked and accordingly the value of variable **level** is set. This is shown in the code below.

```
if ( digitalRead ( high_level ) == LOW && digitalRead ( med_level ) ==
    LOW && digitalRead ( low_level ) == LOW )
{
    level = 0 ;
}

if ( digitalRead ( high_level ) == LOW && digitalRead ( med_level ) ==
    LOW  && digitalRead ( low_level ) == HIGH )
```

```
{
    level = 1 ;
}

if ( digitalRead ( high_level ) == LOW && digitalRead ( med_level ) ==
    HIGH && digitalRead ( low_level ) == HIGH )
{
    level = 2 ;
}

if ( digitalRead ( high_level ) == HIGH && digitalRead ( med_level ) ==
    HIGH && digitalRead ( low_level ) == HIGH )
{
    level = 3 ;
}
```

The **level** value is magnified by multiplying it by a fixed value, so that it can be plotted on the ThingSpeak graph. The **level** value is converted to a string before sending it to ThingSpeak. The value is also printed on the display monitor.

The TCP connection is established with the ThingSpeak server (api.thingspeak.com) at port 80 using the command "AT+CIPSTART". If an error occurs, it is shown on the display monitor using the following code:

```
String cmd = "AT+CIPSTART=\"TCP\",\"" ;
cmd += "184.106.153.149" ; // api.thingspeak.com
cmd += "\",80" ;
ser.println ( cmd ) ;
if ( ser.find ( "Error" ) )
{
    Serial.println ( "AT+CIPSTART error" ) ;
    return ;
}
```

The GET string is prepared for sending temperature data to the ThingSpeak server using HTTP 1.1 protocol. The code that achieves this is shown below:

```
String getStr = "GET /update?api_key=" ;
getStr += apiKey ;
```

Experiment 18: Water Level Monitor

```
getStr +="&field1=" ;
getStr += String ( strTemp ) ;
getStr += "\r\n\r\n" ;
```

The "AT+CIPSEND" command and the length of the data are now sent to the server. In the response from server, ">" is searched. If it is found the string **getStr** is sent to the server. If ">" is not found, then it's an error and the connection with server is closed. This is shown below:

```
cmd = "AT+CIPSEND=" ;
cmd += String ( getStr.length( ) ) ;
ser.println ( cmd ) ;

if ( esp8266.find ( ">" ) )
{
    ser.print ( getStr ) ;
}
else
{
    ser.println ( "AT+CIPCLOSE" ) ;
    Serial.println ( "AT+CIPCLOSE" ) ;
}
```

Functions Used

The functions used in this experiment are already covered in previous Experiments.

More Tweaks

1. Connect a LCD display to Arduino and develop a sketch to monitor water level on continuous basis. Show the water level on a LCD display.
2. Connect buzzer on Application board and develop a sketch to raise alarm sound when the water level is high.

EXPERIMENT NINETEEN

MULTI COLOR LED CONTROL

The whole world, as we experience it visually, comes to us through the mystic realm of color.

- *Hans Hofmann*

224　　　　　　　　　　　　　　　21 IoT Experiments

Experiment

This Experiment is about controlling a multi-color LED over Internet / Intranet so that it emits different colored light using a web interface.

Hardware Setup

This Experiment needs an ESP-8266 board, Multi Color LED and Arduino Uno board. These are shown in Figures 19.1, 19.2 and 19.3.

Figure 19.1 ESP-8266 Board

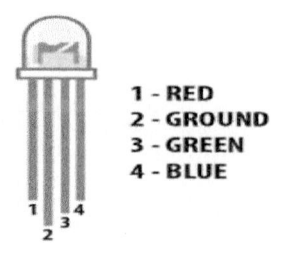

1 - RED
2 - GROUND
3 - GREEN
4 - BLUE

Figure 19.2 Multi Color LED

Experiment 19 : Multi Color LED control **225**

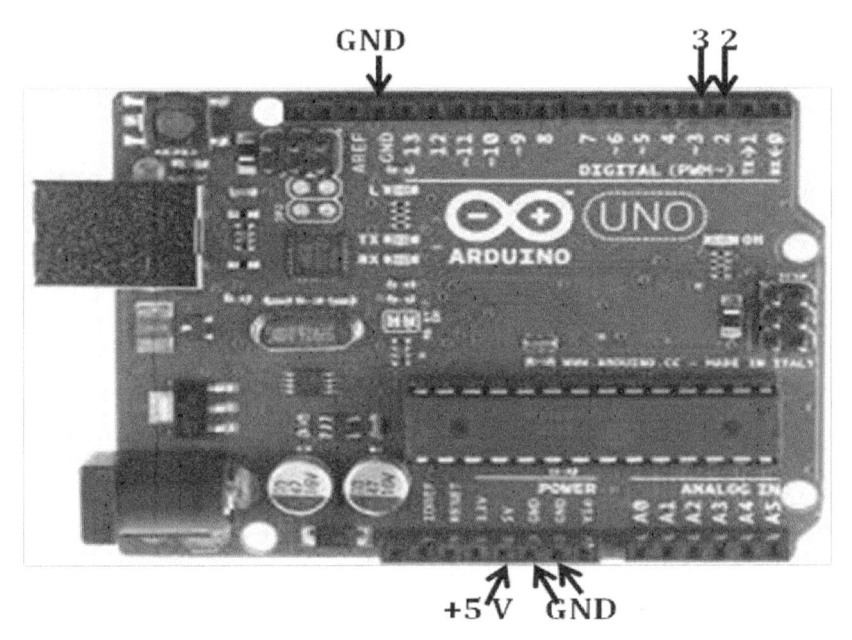

Figure 19.3 Arduino Uno

Pin connections shown in Figure 19.4 should be made.

Arduino Pins	ESP-8266 Board Pins
Digital pin 2	TX
Digital pin 3	RX
+5V	+5V
GND	GND

21 IoT Experiments

Arduino Pins	Multi-colored LED
GND	Pin 2 (GROUND)
Digital pin 9	Pin 4 (Blue)
Digital pin 10	Pin 3 (Green)
Digital pin 11	Pin 1 (Red)

Figure 19.4 Pin connections

Software Setup

Prepare a HTML page with four buttons. The page also includes a jquery library. The jquery library is required to handle button clicks. The library sends HTTP requests to ESP-8266 module. Refer the "Software Setup" steps of Experiment "Internet / Intranet Based LED Control" for jquery library download and setup.

Set the IP address of ESP-8266 module correctly in the html file. This is a very important step. The HTTP request is sent to this IP address and hence it must be ensured that it is set correctly.

HTML Code

```
<html>
   <head>
      <title>MultiColor LED Control</title>
   </head>
   <body>

         <!-- in <button> tags, ID attribute is value sent to the arduino -->

         <button id="10" class="rgbled">Blue</button>
         <button id="11" class="rgbled">Green</button>
         <button id="12" class="rgbled">Red</button>
         <button id="13" class="rgbled">Yellow</button>
         <button id="14" class="rgbled">Pink</button>
```

Experiment 19 : Multi Color LED control

```html
<script src="jquery-1.10.2.min.js"></script>
<script type="text/javascript">
$ ( document ) .ready ( function( ) {
    // alert ( "inside ready" ) ;
} ) ;

$ ( ".rgbled" ) .click ( function( ) {
    // get id value ( i.e. pin10, 11, 12, 13, 14 )
    var p = $ ( this ) .attr ( 'id' ) ;
    // send HTTP GET request to IP address with parameter
    // "pin" and value "p"
    $.get ( "http:// 192.168.1.4:80/", {pin:p} ) ; // GET request
} ) ;

</script>
</body>
</html>
```

Sketch

```
// Multi Color LED control
#include <SoftwareSerial.h>
#define DEBUG true

// Connect the TX line from the esp to the Arduino's pin 2
// Connect the RX line from the esp to the Arduino's pin 3
SoftwareSerial esp8266 ( 2, 3 ) ;

void setup( )
{
    Serial.begin ( 9600 ) ;
    esp8266.begin ( 9600 ) ;
    Serial.println ( "Ready!!" ) ;

    // Blue lead of RGB LED
    pinMode ( 9, OUTPUT ) ;
    digitalWrite ( 9, LOW ) ;
```

```
    // Green lead of RGB LED
    pinMode ( 10, OUTPUT ) ;
    digitalWrite ( 10, LOW ) ;

    // Red lead of RGB LED
    pinMode ( 11, OUTPUT ) ;
    digitalWrite ( 11, LOW ) ;

    // reset module
    sendData ( "AT+RST\r\n", 2000, DEBUG ) ;
    // configure as access point as well as station
    sendData ( "AT+CWMODE=3\r\n", 1000, DEBUG ) ;
    // Connect to your access point, type your own SSID and password
    sendData ( "AT+CWJAP=\"UTkorde\", \"XXXXXX\"\r\n", 5000,
            DEBUG ) ;
    delay ( 3000 ) ;
    // get ip address
    sendData ( "AT+CIFSR\r\n", 3000, DEBUG ) ;
    delay ( 1000 ) ;
    // configure for multiple connections
    sendData ( "AT+CIPMUX=1\r\n", 2000, DEBUG ) ;
    // turn on server on port 80
    sendData ( "AT+CIPSERVER=1,80\r\n", 1000, DEBUG ) ;
}

void loop( )
{
    // check if the esp is sending a message
    if ( esp8266.available( ) )
    {
        if ( esp8266.find ( "+IPD," ) )
        {
            // wait for the serial buffer to fill up
            // read all the serial data
            delay ( 1000 ) ;
            // get the connection id so that we can then disconnect
            // subtract 48 because read( ) function returns
            // the ASCII decimal value
            int connectionId = esp8266.read( ) - 48 ;

            // advance cursor to "pin="
```

Experiment 19 : Multi Color LED control **229**

```
esp8266.find ( "pin=" ) ;

// get first digit i.e. if the pin 12 then the 1st digit is 1,
// then multiply to get 10
int pinNumber = ( esp8266.read( ) - 48 ) * 10 ;
// get second digit, i.e. if the pin number is 12 then the
// 2nd digit is 2, then add to the first number
pinNumber += ( esp8266.read( ) - 48 ) ;

// Blue color
if ( pinNumber == 10 )
{
    analogWrite ( 9, 255 ) ;
    analogWrite ( 10, 0 ) ;
    analogWrite ( 11, 0 ) ;
}
// Green color
if ( pinNumber == 11 )
{
    analogWrite ( 9, 0 ) ;
    analogWrite ( 10, 255 ) ;
    analogWrite ( 11, 0 ) ;
}
// Red color
if ( pinNumber == 12 )
{
    analogWrite ( 9, 0 ) ;
    analogWrite ( 10, 0 ) ;
    analogWrite ( 11, 255 ) ;
}
// Yellow color
if ( pinNumber == 13 )
{
    analogWrite ( 9, 0 ) ;
    analogWrite ( 10, 128 ) ;
    analogWrite ( 11, 128 ) ;
}
// Pink color
if ( pinNumber == 14 )
{
    analogWrite ( 9, 204 ) ;
```

```
            analogWrite ( 10, 51 ) ;
            analogWrite ( 11, 255 ) ;
        }

        // make close command
        String closeCommand = "AT+CIPCLOSE=" ;
        // append connection id
        closeCommand += connectionId ;
        closeCommand += "\r\n" ;
        // close connection
        sendData ( closeCommand, 1000, DEBUG ) ;
    }
  }
}

String sendData ( String command, const int timeout, boolean debug )
{
    String response = "" ;
    // send the read character to the esp8266
    esp8266.print ( command ) ;

    long int time = millis( ) ;

    while ( ( time + timeout ) > millis( ) )
    {
        while ( esp8266.available( ) )
        {
            char c = esp8266.read( ) ;
            response += c ;
        }
    }

    if ( debug )
    {
        Serial.print ( response ) ;
    }

    return response ;
}
```

Experiment 19 : Multi Color LED control 231

Result

When the Arduino sketch is run, following things happen:

- Ready message is shown on the display monitor.
- AT commands are shown on the display monitor.
- IP address of ESP-8266 module is shown on the display monitor.
- ESP 8266 is configured as TCP server to receive commands over net on port 80.

Open the HTML page in Browser. Ensure that IP address of ESP-8266 is correctly added to HTML script.

Press the buttons and watch the effect of changing color of the multi-colored LED. Permit a delay of few seconds, before the effect takes place.

Explanation

About html page

In the HTML page the **head** and **body** tags are defined. The **title** tag is used for giving the title of the Experiment. In the body tag 5 buttons are defined with a specific id and with an attribute class. The script is given below:

```
<button id="10" class="rgbled">Blue</button>
<button id="11" class="rgbled">Green</button>
<button id="12" class="rgbled">Red</button>
<button id="13" class="rgbled">Yellow</button>
 <button id="14" class="rgbled">Pink</button>
```

The jquery library is included in the script through the statement

```
<script src="jquery-1.10.2.min.js"></script>
```

The **click( )** function gets invoked when a button is pressed. The class attribute "led" is used to have uniform response for various button clicks. This function uses the attribute "id" for deciding which button has been pressed and accordingly issues a HTTP GET request to the ESP-8266 module. This request is made by calling the **get( )** function. IP address and pin are sent as parameters to **get( )** function. The following part of the HTML script achieves this functionality:

```
$ ( ".rgbled" ) .click ( function( )
{
        // get id value ( i.e. 10, 11, 12, 13, 14 )
        var p = $ ( this ) .attr ( 'id' ) ;
        // send HTTP GET request to the IP address with the parameter
        // "pin" and value "p"
        $.get ( "http:// 192.168.1.4:80/", {pin:p} ) ; // GET request
 });
```

About Arduino sketch

The sketch relies on the Software Serial library. This library allows serial communication to take place on digital pins other than 0 and 1. The sketch uses "SoftwareSerial.h" for communication between Arduino and ESP-8266. Initially, object **esp8266** of SoftwareSerial is created, with pins as 2 and 3 as input to the constructor.

The **setup( )** function initializes serial communication with PC using **Serial.begin( )**. It also sets baud-rate for Software Serial port using **esp8266.begin( )**. The digital pins 9, 10 and 11 are configured as OUTPUT using **pinMode( )** function. The **digitalWrite( )** functions sets these pins to LOW. The method **sendData( )** is used for configuring ESP-8266. Following steps are performed to configure ESP-8266 module before it can be used:

- Reset the ESP-8266 module using AT+RST command.

- Configure the ESP-8266 module to act as Access Point as well as station, using AT+CWMODE=3 command.

- Connect the ESP-8266 module to your Access Point using your SSID and password. The command is AT+CWJAP=<SSID>,<password>.

- Get the IP address of ESP-8266 module using AT+CIFSR command.

Experiment 19 : Multi Color LED control **233**

- Configure the ESP-8266 to have multiple connections. The command is AT+CIPMUX=1.

- Configure the ESP-8266 to act as server with port 80 being used for communication with client. The command is AT+CIPSERVER=1,80.

In the **loop( )** function a check is performed, whether ESP-8266 is sending any message. This can happen when a control command (via HTTP **get( )**) is received by ESP-8266 module. If the message is available, then search for "+IPD," pattern is done. If this succeeds then read is performed to get connection Id. A variable **connnectionId** is used to store the value after subtracting 48 to get the decimal number. Then reading is advanced to find "pin=" pattern. The following code achieves this:

```
if ( esp8266.find ( "+IPD," ) )
{
    delay ( 1000 ) ;
    int connectionId = esp8266.read( ) - 48 ;
    esp8266.find ( "pin=" ) ;
    ...
}
```

The pin number is read in the variable **pinNumber**. This is done in two steps. Firstly, most significant digit is read and is multiplied by 10 to get ten's digit. This is followed by reading unit's place digit and sum is performed to obtain the actual pin number. This is achieved through the following statements:

```
int pinNumber = ( esp8266.read( ) - 48 ) * 10 ;
pinNumber += ( esp8266.read( ) - 48 ) ;
```

The different colors are generated using various combinations of Red, Green and Blue values. The method **analogWrite( )** is used to write various values. The colors that are expected to be generated are Blue, Green, Red, Yellow and Pink. This is achieved through the code given below.

```
// Blue color
if ( pinNumber == 10 )
{
```

```
    analogWrite ( 9, 255 ) ;
    analogWrite ( 10, 0 ) ;
    analogWrite ( 11, 0 ) ;
}
// Green Color
if ( pinNumber == 11 )
{
    analogWrite ( 9, 0 ) ;
    analogWrite ( 10, 255 ) ;
    analogWrite ( 11, 0 ) ;
}
// Red Color
if ( pinNumber == 12 )
{
    analogWrite ( 9, 0 ) ;
    analogWrite ( 10, 0 ) ;
    analogWrite ( 11, 255 ) ;
}
// Yellow color
if ( pinNumber == 13 )
{
    analogWrite ( 9, 0 ) ;
    analogWrite ( 10, 128 ) ;
    analogWrite ( 11, 128 ) ;
}
// Pink color
if ( pinNumber == 14 )
{
    analogWrite ( 9, 204 ) ;
    analogWrite ( 10, 51 ) ;
    analogWrite ( 11, 255 ) ;
}
```

Finally, the connection is closed by issuing close command using **connectionId**.

Functions Used

The functions used in this Experiment are already covered in previous Experiments.

Experiment 19 : Multi Color LED control **235**

More Tweaks

1. Enhance the Experiment by developing an Arduino sketch to control multi-color LED and play a melody using buzzer of the Application board. A different melody should be played for each of the color displayed.

2. Develop an Arduino sketch to control multi-color LED and display the name of the color on LCD display, corresponding to the color of multi-color LED.

CHAPTER TWENTY

INTERNET / INTRANET BASED MOTOR SPEED CONTROL

There is more to life than increasing its speed.
- *Mahatma Gandhi*

Experiment

This Experiment is about controlling speed of DC motor over Internet / Intranet using a web interface.

Hardware Setup

This Experiment needs an ESP-8266 board, Motor Driver board with DC motor and Arduino Uno board. These are shown in Figures 20.1, 20.2 and 20.3.

Figure 20.1 ESP-8266 Board

Figure 20.2 Motor driver board and DC motor

Experiment 19: Intranet based Motor Speed Control **239**

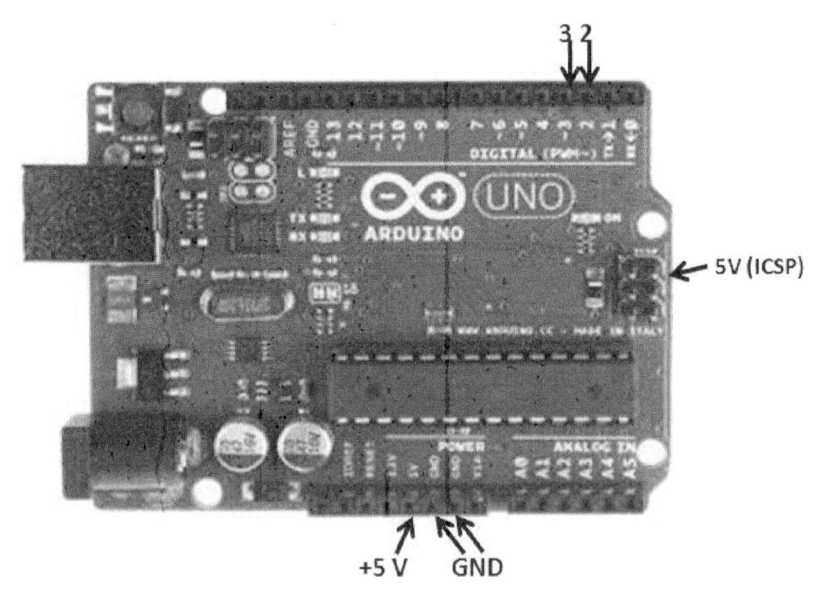

Figure 20.3 Arduino Uno

Pin connections shown in Figure 20.4 should be made.

Arduino Pins	Motor Driver Board Pins
Vin	+12V
Digital pin 4	IN 1
Digital pin 5	IN 2
+5V	+5V
GND	GND

Arduino Pins	ESP-8266 Board Pins
Digital pin 2	TX
Digital pin 3	RX
5V (ICSP pin)	+5V
GND	GND

Motor Driver Board Pins	DC Motor
LEFT (+)	Red wire (Terminal 1)
LEFT (-)	Black wire (Terminal 2)

Figure 19.4 Pin connections

Connect Power Adapter to the Arduino Uno board (or insert batteries in the battery holder and connect). Switch it ON so that external supply is provided. This is required for motor driver board to drive the DC motor.

Software Setup

Prepare a HTML page with four buttons. The pages also include a jquery library. The jquery library is required to handle button clicks. The library sends HTTP requests to ESP-8266 module. Refer the "Software Setup" steps of Experiment "Internet / Intranet Based LED Control" for jquery library download and setup.

Set the IP address of ESP-8266 module correctly in the HTML file. This is very important step. The HTTP request is sent to this IP address and hence it must be ensured that it is set correctly.

Experiment 19: Intranet based Motor Speed Control 241

HTML Code

```html
<html>
   <head>
      <title>Motor Speed Control</title>
   </head>
   <body>

      <!-- in <button> tags, ID attribute is value sent to the arduino -->
      <button id="11" class="motor">HIGH Speed</button>
      <button id="12" class="motor">MED Speed</button>
      <button id="13" class="motor">LOW Speed</button>

      <script src="jquery-1.10.2.min.js"></script>
      <script type="text/javascript">
      $ ( document ) .ready ( function( ) {
          // alert ( "inside ready" ) ;
      } ) ;

      $ ( ".motor" ) .click ( function( ) {
            // get id value ( i.e. pin 11, 12, 13 )
            var p = $ ( this ) .attr ( 'id' ) ;
            // alert ( p ) ;

      // send HTTP GET request to the IP address with the parameter
      // "pin" and value "p"
      $.get ( "http:// 192.168.1.4:80/", {pin:p} ) ; // GET request
         } ) ;
      </script>
   </body>
</html>
```

Sketch

```
// Motor speed control
#include <SoftwareSerial.h>
#define DEBUG true
```

```
// Connect the TX line from the esp to the Arduino's pin 2
// Connect the RX line from the esp to the Arduino's pin 3
SoftwareSerial esp8266 ( 2, 3 ) ;

void setup( )
{
    Serial.begin ( 9600 ) ;
    esp8266.begin ( 9600 ) ;
    Serial.println ( "Ready!!" ) ;

    // motor pin
    pinMode ( 5, OUTPUT ) ;
    digitalWrite ( 5, LOW ) ;

    // motor pin
    pinMode ( 4, OUTPUT ) ;
    digitalWrite ( 4, LOW ) ;

    // reset module
    sendData ( "AT+RST\r\n", 2000, DEBUG ) ;
    // configure as access point as well as station
    sendData ( "AT+CWMODE=3\r\n", 1000, DEBUG ) ;
    // Connect to your access point, type your own SSID and password
    sendData ( "AT+CWJAP=\"UTkorde\", \"XXXXXX\"\r\n", 5000,
            DEBUG ) ;
    delay ( 3000 ) ;
    // get ip address
    sendData ( "AT+CIFSR\r\n", 3000, DEBUG ) ;
    delay ( 1000 ) ;
    // configure for multiple connections
    sendData ( "AT+CIPMUX=1\r\n", 2000, DEBUG ) ;
    // turn on server on port 80
    sendData ( "AT+CIPSERVER=1,80\r\n", 1000, DEBUG ) ;
}

void loop( )
{
    // check if the esp is sending a message
    if ( esp8266.available( ) )
    {
        if ( esp8266.find ( "+IPD," ) )
```

Experiment 19: Intranet based Motor Speed Control

```
{
    // wait for the serial buffer to fill up
    // read all the serial data
    delay ( 1000 ) ;
    // get the connection id so that we can then disconnect
    // subtract 48 because the read( ) function returns
    int connectionId = esp8266.read( ) - 48 ;

    // advance cursor to "pin="
    esp8266.find ( "pin=" ) ;

    // get first digit i.e. if the pin 13 then the 1st digit is 1,
    // then multiply to get 10
    int pinNumber = ( esp8266.read( ) - 48 ) * 10 ;
    // get second digit, i.e. if the pin number is 13 then the
    // 2nd digit is 3, then add to the first number
    pinNumber += ( esp8266.read( ) - 48 ) ;

    // high speed
    if ( pinNumber == 11 )
    {
        analogWrite ( 5, 255 ) ;
        digitalWrite ( 4, LOW ) ;
    }

    // medium speed
    if ( pinNumber == 12 )
    {
        analogWrite ( 5, 180 ) ;
        digitalWrite ( 4, LOW ) ;
    }

    // low speed
    if ( pinNumber == 13 )
    {
        analogWrite ( 5, 100 ) ;
        digitalWrite ( 4, LOW ) ;
    }

    // make close command
    String closeCommand = "AT+CIPCLOSE=" ;
```

```
            // append connection id
            closeCommand += connectionId ;
            closeCommand += "\r\n" ;

            // close connection
            sendData ( closeCommand, 1000, DEBUG ) ;
        }
    }
}

String sendData ( String command, const int timeout, boolean debug )
{
    String response = "" ;
    // send the read character to the esp8266
    esp8266.print ( command ) ;

    long int time = millis( ) ;

    while ( ( time + timeout ) > millis( ) )
    {
        while ( esp8266.available( ) )
        {
            // The esp has data so display its output to the serial window
            // read the next character
            char c = esp8266.read( ) ;
            response += c ;
        }
    }

    if ( debug )
    {
        Serial.print ( response ) ;
    }

    return response ;
}
```

Experiment 19: Intranet based Motor Speed Control 245

Result

When the Arduino sketch is run, following things happen:

- Ready message is shown on the display monitor.
- AT commands are shown on the display monitor.
- IP address of ESP-8266 module is shown on the display monitor.
- ESP 8266 is configured as TCP server to receive commands over net on port 80.

Open the HTML page in Browser. Ensure that IP address of ESP-8266 is correctly added to HTML script.

Press the buttons one watch the effect of changing speed as you press the various buttons. Permit a delay of few seconds, before the effect takes place.

Explanation

About html page

In the html page the **head** and **body** tags are defined. The **title** tag is used for giving the title of the Experiment. In the **body** tag 3 buttons are defined with a specific id and with an attribute class. The script is given below:

```
<button id="11" class="motor">HIGH Speed</button>
<button id="12" class="motor">MED Speed</button>
<button id="13" class="motor">LOW Speed</button>
```

The jquery library is included in the script through the statement

```
<script src="jquery-1.10.2.min.js"></script>
```

The **click( )** gets invoked when a button is pressed. The class attribute "**motor**" is used to have uniform response for various button clicks. This function uses the attribute "id" for deciding which button has been pressed and accordingly issues a HTTP GET request to the ESP-8266 module. This request is made by calling the **get( )** function. IP address and pin are sent as parameters to **get( )** function. The following part of the HTML script achieves this functionality:

```
$ ( ".motor" ) .click ( function( ) {
        // get id value ( i.e. pin 11, 12, 13 )
        var p = $ ( this ) .attr ( 'id' ) ;
        // send HTTP GET request to the IP address with the parameter
        // "pin" and value "p"
        $.get ( "http:// 192.168.1.4:80/", {pin:p} ) ; // GET request
}) ;
```

About Arduino sketch

The sketch relies on the Software Serial library. This library allows serial communication to take place on digital pins other than 0 and 1. The sketch uses "SoftwareSerial.h" for communication between Arduino and ESP-8266. Initially, object **esp8266** of SoftwareSerial is created, with pins as 2 and 3 as input to the constructor.

The **setup( )** function initializes serial communication with PC using **Serial.begin( )**. It also sets baud rate for Software Serial port using **esp8266.begin( )**. The digital pins 4 and 5 are configured as OUTPUT using **pinMode( )** function. The **digitalWrite( )** functions sets these pins to LOW. The method **sendData( )** is used for configuring ESP-8266. Following steps are performed to configure ESP-8266 module before it can be used:

- Reset the ESP-8266 module using AT+RST command.

- Configure the ESP-8266 module to act as Access Point as well as station, using AT+CWMODE=3 command.

- Connect the ESP-8266 module to your Access Point using your SSID and password. The command is AT+CWJAP=<SSID>,<password>.

- Get the IP address of ESP-8266 module using AT+CIFSR command.

- Configure the ESP-8266 to have multiple connections. The command is AT+CIPMUX=1.

Experiment 19: Intranet based Motor Speed Control **247**

- Configure the ESP-8266 to act as server with port 80 being used for communication with client. The command is AT+CIPSERVER=1,80.

In the **loop( )** function, the check is performed, whether ESP-8266 is sending any message. This can happen when a control command (via HTTP **get( )**) is received by ESP-8266 module. If the message is available, then search for "+IPD," pattern is done. If this succeeds then read is performed to get connection Id. A variable **connnectionId** is used to store the value after subtracting 48 to get the decimal number. Then reading is advanced to find "pin=" pattern. The following code achieves this:

```
if ( esp8266.find ( "+IPD," ) )
{
    delay ( 1000 );
    int connectionId = esp8266.read( ) - 48 ;
    esp8266.find ( "pin=" );
    ...
}
```

The pin number is read in the variable **pinNumber**. This is done in two steps. Firstly, most significant digit is read and is multiplied by 10 to get ten's digit. This is followed by reading unit's place digit and sum is performed to obtain the actual pin number. This is achieved through the following statements:

```
int pinNumber = ( esp8266.read( ) - 48 ) * 10 ;
pinNumber += ( esp8266.read( ) - 48 ) ;
```

Different speeds are set for each button pressed. The **analogWrite( )** function is used to set different value for pin 5. This allows the motor to rotate at different speed. Pin 4 is held at LOW using **digitalWrite( )**. This is achieved through the code given below:

```
// high speed
if ( pinNumber == 11 )
{
    analogWrite ( 5, 255 );
    digitalWrite ( 4, LOW );
}
```

```
// medium speed
if ( pinNumber == 12 )
{
    analogWrite ( 5, 180 ) ;
    digitalWrite ( 4, LOW ) ;
}

// low speed
if ( pinNumber == 13 )
{
    analogWrite ( 5, 100 ) ;
    digitalWrite ( 4, LOW ) ;
}
```

Finally, the connection is closed by issuing close command using **connectionId**.

Functions Used

The functions used in this Experiment are already covered in previous Experiments.

More Tweaks

Enhance the Experiment by developing an Arduino sketch and HTML page, to control direction of motor rotation. Have two buttons on web page—Clockwise and Anti-Clockwise.

EXPERIMENT
TWENTY ONE

SOIL MOISTURE MONITOR AND SD-CARD LOGGER

Keep the soil healthy and the bad seed won't grow.
- *David Agus*

Experiment

This Experiment is about monitoring soil moisture of the area where trees are planted. The soil moisture is logged to a SD-Card. This helps to take care of plants using history of soil moisture readings.

Hardware Setup

In addition to Arduino Uno board this Experiment needs a Soil moisture sensor along with its driver board called, SD Card board and. These are shown in Figures 21.3, 21.1 and 21.2.

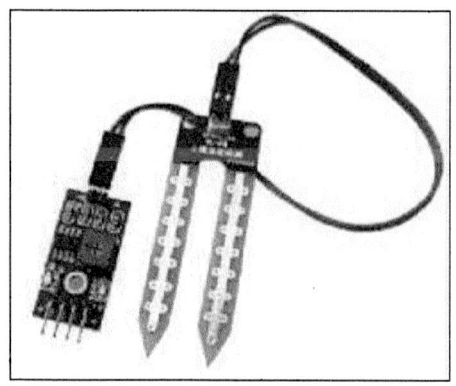

Figure 21.1 Soil moisture and driver board

Figure 21.2 SD Card board

Experiment 21: Soil Moisture monitor & SD-Card Logger 251

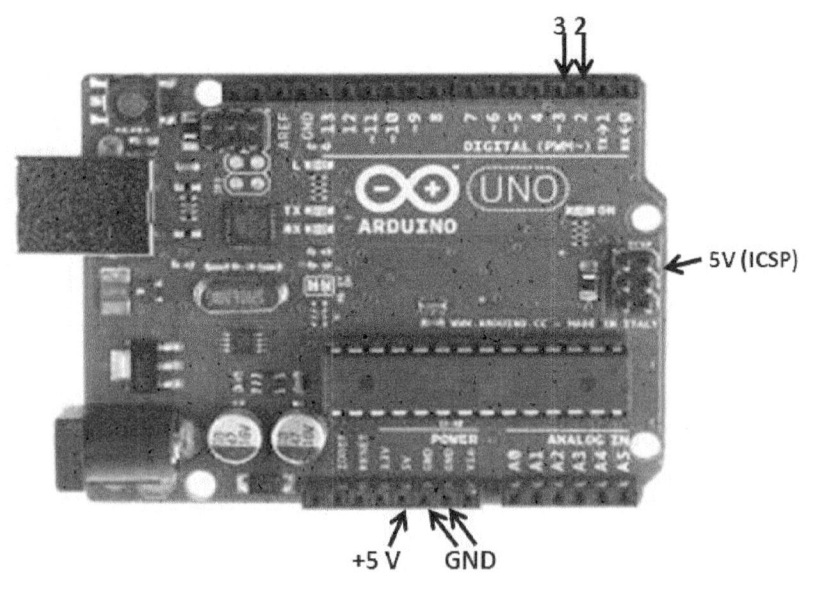

Figure 21.3 Arduino Uno

Pin connections shown in Figure 21.4 should be made.

Arduino Pins	SD Card Board
Digital pin 10	CS pin
Digital pin 11	MOSI pin
Digital pin 12	MISO (MOSO) pin
Digital pin 13	SCK pin
5V (ICSP pin)	VCC
GND	GND

Arduino Pins	Moosture Sensor Board
Analog pin (A0)	AO (analog output value)
Digital pin 3	RX
+5V	VCC
GND	GND

Figure 19.4 Pin connections

Connect Power Adapter to the Arduino Uno board (or insert batteries in the battery holder and connect). Switch it ON so that external supply is provided.

Sketch

```
// Moisture monitor and logger to SDcard

#include <stdlib.h>
#include <SPI.h>
#include <SD.h>
#define MAX_READINGS 10

// Moisture Sensor pin
// Analog pin A0
int Moisture = A0 ;
static int readingsCounter = 0 ;
// File instance
File myFile ;
int CS_PIN = 10 ;
String fileName = "test.txt" ;

/* SD card attached to SPI bus as follows
 ** MOSI - pin 11
 ** MISO ( MOSO ) - pin 12
 ** CLK ( SCK ) - pin 13
 ** CS - pin 10
 */
```

Experiment 21: Soil Moisture monitor & SD-Card Logger

```
// this runs once
void setup( )
{
    // enable debug serial
    Serial.begin ( 9600 ) ;

    Serial.print ( "Initializing SD card..." ) ;
    if ( !SD.begin ( CS_PIN ) )
    {
        Serial.println ( "Initialization failed!" ) ;
    }
    else
    {
        Serial.println ( "Initialization done." ) ;
    }
    // open the file for writing moisture readings
    myFile = SD.open ( fileName, FILE_WRITE ) ;
    delay ( 2000 ) ;
    if ( !myFile )
    {
        Serial.println ( "Error opening file to write" ) ;
    }
}

// the loop
void loop( )
{
    // read the value from Moisture Sensor.
    // read 10 values for averaging.
    int val = 0 ;
    for ( int i = 0 ; i < 10 ; i++ )
    {
        val += analogRead ( Moisture ) ;
        delay ( 500 ) ;
    }

    // Store value into temp variable:
    float temp = val / 10 ;
    // convert to string
    String strTemp = String ( temp, 1 ) ;
    // print readings on display monitor
```

```
Serial.println ( strTemp ) ;

if ( myFile && ( readingsCounter < MAX_READINGS ) )
{
    // increment reading counter
    readingsCounter ++ ;
    // write to the file
    myFile.println ( strTemp ) ;
}
if ( readingsCounter == MAX_READINGS )
{
    // close the file
    myFile.close( ) ;

    // re-open the file for reading
    myFile = SD.open ( fileName ) ;
    if ( myFile )
    {
        Serial.println ( "Reading from " + fileName + ":" ) ;

        // read from the file until there's nothing else in it
        while ( myFile.available( ) )
        {
            Serial.write ( myFile.read( ) ) ;
            delay ( 100 ) ;
        }
        // close the file after reading is done
        myFile.close( ) ;
        Serial.println ( "Reading from file done.." ) ;
    }
    else
    {
        // if the file didn't open, print an error
        Serial.println ( "error opening file to read" ) ;
    }
    // wait in loop as reading of file is done
    while ( true ) ;
}
}
```

Result

When the Arduino sketch is run, following things happen:

- The soil moisture values are shown in the serial monitor (Ensure that moisture sensor is inserted in wet soil).
- The moisture values are written to SD Card. Ensure that SD card is inserted in the SD Card board.
- The written values are read from SD Card and displayed on the serial monitor.

Explanation

The sketch makes use of the SD card library. This library allows I/O from/to a SD card. The communication between Microcontroller on Arduino board and the SD card uses SPI interface (Serial Peripheral Interface). The header files required to access SD card are "SD.h" and "SPI.h". The SD library uses digital pins 11, 12 and 13 and digital pin 10 as CS (Chip Select) to interact with the SD card.

The sketch uses a variable **Moisture** to read soil moisture readings on analog pin A0. The variable **readingsCounter** is used as counter for taking moisture readings. The variable **CS_PIN** acts as Chip Select and Digital pin 10 is used for it. A FILE instance **myFIle** is used to perform file operations. The file name is stored in variable **filename**.

The **setup( )** function initializes serial communication with PC using **Serial.begin( )**. The initialization of SD card is done via **SD.begin( )** function call. A file is opened for writing moisture readings using **SD.open( )** function as given below.

```
myFile = SD.open ( fileName, FILE_WRITE ) ;
if ( !myFile )
{
    Serial.println ( "error opening file to write" ) ;
}
```

In the **loop( )** function, the moisture readings are taken using **analogRead( )**. Multiple readings are taken in a **for** loop and then an average value is calculated, so that a stable value is obtained. The value is converted into string so that it can be sent over Internet to ThingSpeak and be written to a file. This value is also displayed on the display monitor. The following code gives this:

```
int val = 0 ;
for ( int i = 0 ; i < 10 ; i++ )
{
    val += analogRead ( Moisture ) ;
    delay ( 500 ) ;
}
float temp = val / 10 ;
String strTemp = String ( temp, 1 ) ;
Serial.println ( strTemp ) ;
```

The readings are written to a file till **readingsCounter** value is less than MAX_READINGS. The following code snippet gives this:

```
if ( myFile && ( readingsCounter < MAX_READINGS ) )
{
    readingsCounter ++ ;
    myFile.println ( strTemp ) ;
}
```

When **readingsCounter** reaches MAX_READINGS, the file is closed. The file is re-opened for reading using **SD.open( )**. The file is read till the data is available. After reading is over, the file is again closed. This is achieved through the following code:

```
if ( readingsCounter == MAX_READINGS )
{
    myFile.close( ) ;
    myFile = SD.open ( fileName ) ;
    if ( myFile )
    {
        Serial.println ( "Reading from " + fileName + ":" ) ;
        while ( myFile.available( ) )
        {
            Serial.write ( myFile.read( ) ) ;
```

Experiment 21: Soil Moisture monitor & SD-Card Logger

```
            delay ( 100 ) ;
        }
        myFile.close( ) ;
        Serial.println ( "Reading from file done.." ) ;
    }
    ...
}
```

Functions Used

Given below is a list of functions that have been used in this Experiment's sketch.

SD.begin (pin)
Initializes the SD library and card. It begins use of SPI bus on a pin.
Return: true on success, false on failure.

SD.open (filename), SD.open (filename, mode)
Opens a file on the SD card. If the file is opened for writing, it will be created if it doesn't already exist.
filename: Name the file to open. Can be path of a file with directories delimited by /.
Return: **File** object referring to the opened file. If failure, object would be set to false.
mode (optional) : defaults to FILE_READ.
FILE_READ: Opens file for reading, start at the beginning of the file.
FILE_WRITE: Opens file for reading and writing starting at the end of the file.

File class read( )
Reads a character from the file.
Usage: myFile.read( ) ;
myFile: Instance of the **File** class returned by **SD.open( )**.
Return: The next byte (or character), -1 if none is available.

File class print( ), println( )
Prints data to the file, which must have been opened for writing. Prints numbers as a sequence of digits, each digit as an ASCII character.
Usage: myFile.write (data) ;
myFile: Instance of the **File** class returned by **SD.open( )**.
data: Data to print (char, byte, int, long, or string).
Return: Number of bytes written.
File class close( )
Closes the file, and ensures that any data written to it is physically saved to the SD card.
Usage: myFile.close( ) ;
myFile: Instance of the **File** class returned by **SD.open( )**.
Return: None.
File class available( )
Checks if there are any bytes available for reading from the file.
Usage: myFile.available( ) ;
myFile: Instance of the **File** class returned by SD.open( ).
Returns: Number of bytes available (int).

More Tweaks

- Enhance the Experiment so that moisture values can be sent over Internet and can be logged to ThingSpeak.
- Enhance the Experiment to display the moisture values on LCD panel and make an automatic plant watering device by connecting a relay board which in turn controls a small water pump.

APPENDIX ONE

ARDUINO PINS AND CONCEPTS

Our Age of Anxiety is, in great part, the result of trying to do today's job with yesterday's tools and yesterday's concepts.

- *Marshall McLuhan*

This chapter provides an overview of the Arduino pins and some of the concepts related to using Arduino. This knowledge is required to make the Experiments successful. Given below is a snapshot of Arduino Uno board.

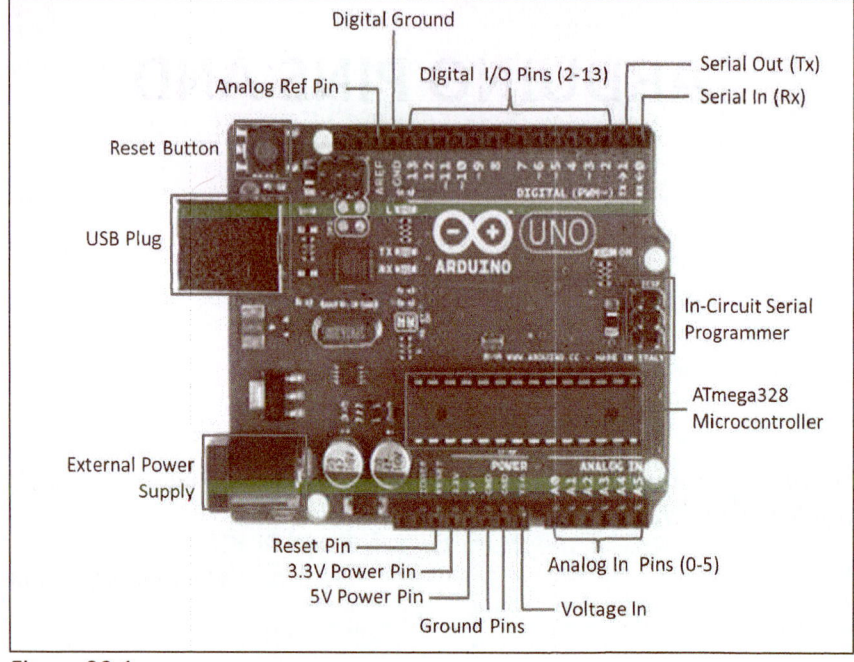

Figure 22.1

Pins Overview

Power Pins

- VIN: The input voltage to the Arduino board when it's using an external power source. VIN range → 9V to 12V.
- 5V: Power supply to power the Arduino board. This is Supplied by USB (or from VIN via an on-board regulator).
- 3.3V: A 3.3 volt supply generated by the on-board regulator. Maximum current draw is 50 mA.
- GND : Ground pins.

Digital Pins

- There are 14 digital pins (0 -13). They can be used as Input or Output.
- Digital pins correspond to discrete values, e.g. 1, 0 are digital values. Its voltage representation is +5V, 0V.

Serial Pins

- Pin 0 (RX) and pin 1 (TX).
- Used to receive (RX) and transmit (TX) serial data. These pins are connected to the corresponding pins of the ATmega8U2 USB-to-Serial chip.

PWM (Pulse Width Modulation)

- Pins 3, 5, 6, 9, 10 and 11.
- Provide 8-bit PWM output (using the **analogWrite( )** function).
- Marked with ~ sign on Arduino board.

Analog Inputs

- 6 pins: A0-A5 inputs.
- They measure from 0 volts to 5 volts.
- Each pin provides equivalent digital value. The digital value has 10-bit resolution.
- 0V at analog pin maps to 0 value, +5V at analog pin maps to 1023. Voltage between 0V to 5V will map to a value between 0 to 1023.

SPI (Serial Peripheral Interface)

- Pins supporting SPI communication, Pins: 10 (SS), 11 (MOSI), 12 (MISO), 13 (SCK).

I2C (Inter Integrated Circuit)

- A04, A05 is used for I2C communication.
- Pin 4 (SDA) and pin 5 (SCL).
- Support I2C communication using the Wire library.

External Interrupts

- Pins: 2 and 3.
- These pins can be configured to trigger an interrupt.

Reset

- Reset can be done in two ways, using the reset button on the Arduino board or connecting external reset button to the pin labeled "RESET".

LED (Built-in LED)

- Pin 13, built-in LED connected to digital pin 13.
- Pin is HIGH value →LED is on.
- Pin is LOW → LED is off.

Concepts

Pull Up Resistors

When a switch is used in a digital circuit, it normally has two states ON and OFF. However, there is third state that is called floating which is neither ON nor OFF. Figure 22.2 depicts the floating point concept. When Switch S is closed, voltage at point B is 5V. So, 5V is applied to the microcontroller. When S is open, point B is neither at 5V or GND. If any stray voltage (or current) is present then the state of microcontroller is not known. It can be ON or OFF and microcontroller might misbehave. So point B is called floating point.

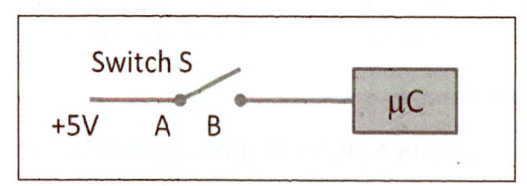

Figure 22.2 Floating Concept

To solve the floating point problem, a pull-up resistor is used. Figure 22.3 shows the concept and use of pull-up resistor. When Switch S is open, voltage at point B is 5V. When S is closed, voltage at point B is GND. This happens because current takes low resistance path to GND. The resistor R acts as limiting resistor. It pulls point B to 5V when S is open.

Arduino Pins and Concepts **263**

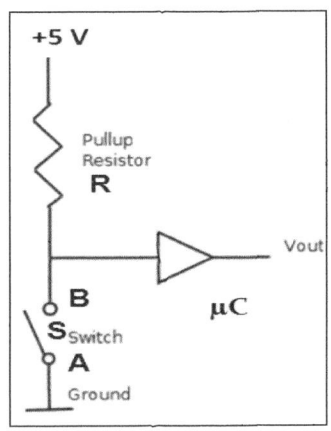

Figure 22.3 Pull-up Resistor

The pull up resistor is normally built into microcontroller (AVR 328) of Arduino Uno as on-chip resistor. It limits the current and protects the chip. To enable pull-up resistor Arduino provides the function

pinMode (pin, INPUT_PULLUP) ;

PWM

Pulse Width Modulation (PWM) is a technique for getting analog results with digital means. A square wave (On and Off) is created using digital control.

The duration of "on time" is called the pulse width. On-Off pattern creates a voltage waveform in between 5 V (On) and 0V (Off). This happens by changing the portion of the time the signal spends On against the time that the signal spends Off. To get varying analog values, we need to change (or modulate) the pulse width. The duration or period is the inverse of the PWM frequency.

The function **analogWrite (pin, value)** is used to generate PWM. This function takes value input from 0 to 255. Figure 22.4 shows PWM examples for different duty cycles.

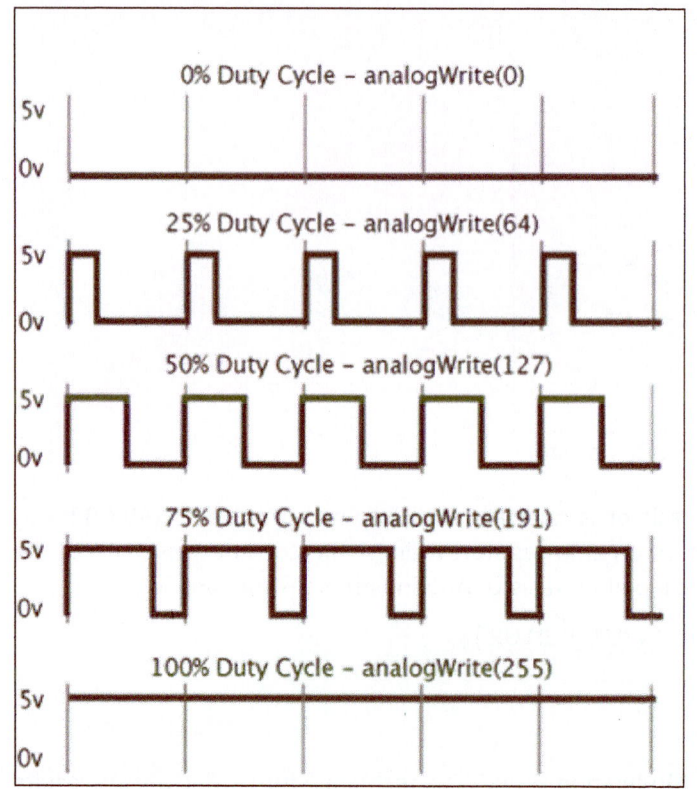

Figure 22.4 Pulse Width Modulation

SPI

Serial Peripheral Interface (SPI) is a synchronous serial data protocol. It's a two-wire protocol with speed up to 10 Mbps. The RS232 / UARTs is asynchronous Serial interface.

SPI is used by Master Controller (MC) for communicating with one or more peripheral devices quickly over short distances. One master device (MC) controls the peripheral devices. This is shown in the Figure 22.5.

Arduino Pins and Concepts **265**

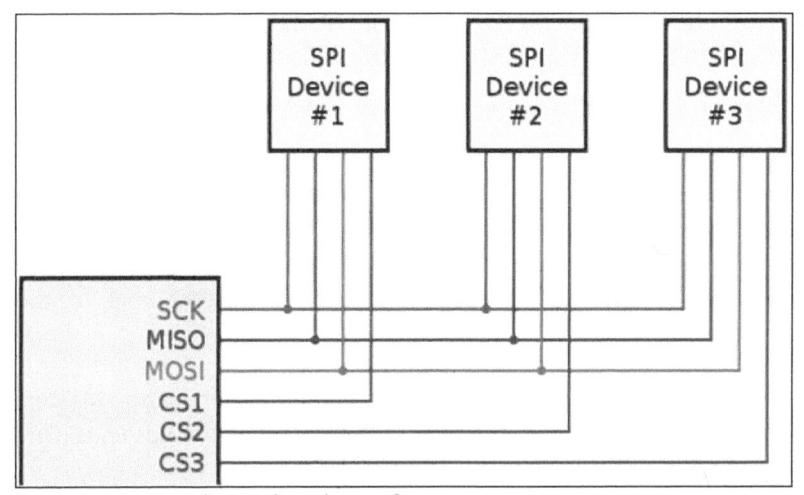

Figure 22.5 Serial Peripheral Interface

The various connection lines of SPI are:

- MISO (Master In Slave Out): Slave line for sending data to the master.
- MOSI (Master Out Slave In): Master line for sending data to peripheral devices.
- SCK (Serial Clock): The clock (synchronize data transmission generated by the master).
- CS /SS (Chip Select or Slave Select): The master can use to enable and disable specific devices.

Arduino Uno is configured for SPI support with following pins:

- Pin 11 → MOSI
- Pin 12 → MISO
- Pin 13 → SCK
- Pin 10 → CS (SS), Digital Pin 10 is preferred. However other pin can also be used, e.g. Digital Pin 4.

I2C

Inter Integrated Circuit (I2C) interface is a two wire interface which can support 1024 devices using 10-bit address, and 128 devices using a 7-bit address. I2C is Multi master system which is a major advance over SPI protocol.

The data rate is in between RS232 and SPI (RS232 < I2C < SPI). The data rates are 100 Kbps (standard), 400 Kbps (fast) and 3.4 Mbps (high speed).

Each peripheral device has a unique address. To ensure smooth exchange of information, Master-Slave protocol is used. Master is a device capable of initiating communication, whereas Slave is a device that obeys the commands generated by the master. The reason why it is called Slave is because; it doesn't play an intelligent role in the communication process.

Master can choose a device it wants to communicate with. Masters can't talk to each other over the bus. Take turns using the bus lines (One master at a time). This is shown in the Figure 22.6.

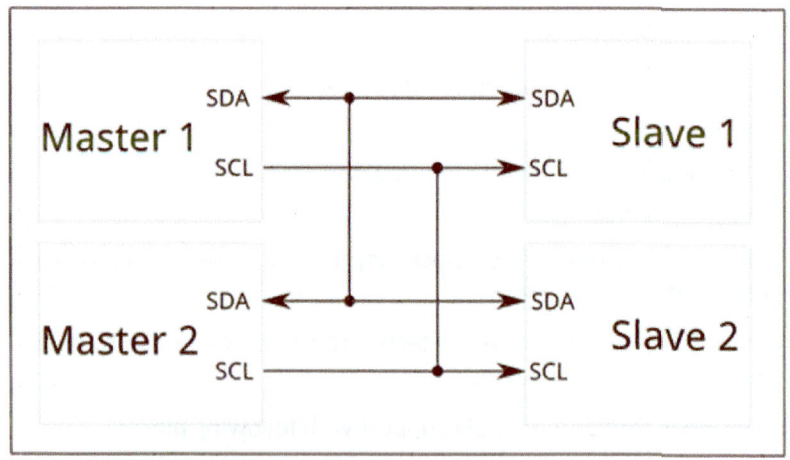

Figure 22.6 Inter Integrated Circuit Interface

Two wires for SPI are:

- SCL - Serial Clock, SCL is used to synchronize data transfer between slave devices. SCL is generated by Master.
- SDA - Serial Data, SDA carries the data.

I2C Support with Arduino Uno:

- Arduino pin A4 has support for SDA.
- Arduino pin A5 support has support for SCL.

KICIT IoT Kit Order Form

Kit contains Hardware Boards, Sensors & Videos of all 21 Experiments

I want to place an order for KICIT IoT Kit. My shipping address is as follows:

Name _____

Address _____

_____

_____

City _____

State _____

PIN _____

Mobile _____

Email _____

1. Please fill in your contact details above and send them to Kanetkar's ICIT Pvt. Ltd., 44-A, Hill Road, Gokulpeth, Nagpur- 440010, India. Or email them to kanetkar@kicit.com.

2. Transfer Rs. 5000/- by NEFT / NetBanking to the following account:

   Bank - HDFC Bank, Dharampeth Extension, Nagpur, India
   Account Name - Kanetkar's ICIT Pvt. Ltd.
   Account Number - 01022260000026
   IFSC Code - HDFC0000102

   OR

3. Prepare a Cheque of Rs. 5000/- in the name of Kanetkar's ICIT Pvt. Ltd. payable at Nagpur and deposit it using above account information into any HDFC Bank branch.

For any query contact Kanetkar's ICIT Pvt. Ltd. at +91-712-2531046, 2545322 or kanetkar@kicit.com